Looking Forward, Looking Backward

Forty Years of Women's Ordination

Edited by Fredrica Harris Thompsett

MP | Morehouse Publishing
NEW YORK · HARRISBURG · DENVER

Morehouse Publishing, 4785 Linglestown Road, Suite 101, Harrisburg, PA 17112
Morehouse Publishing, 19 East 34th Street, New York, NY 10016
Morehouse Publishing is an imprint of Church Publishing Incorporated.

Library of Congress Cataloging-in-Publication Data

A catalog record of this book is available from the Library of Congress:

ISBN-13: 978-0-8192-2922-9 (pbk.)
ISBN-13: 978-0-8192-2923-6 (ebook)

www.churchpublishing.org

An imprint of Church Publishing Incorporated

Cover design by Laurie Klein Westhafer
Typeset by Denise Hoff

Printed in the United States of America

CONTENTS

Setting the Stage[1]

As a participant, the crucifer, in the July 29, 1974, irregular but not invalid ordination of the Philadelphia Eleven—those courageous women and three bishops—at the George W. South Memorial Church of the Advocate, I have several vivid memories of the process set in motion that fateful day. I also am a living witness to what has ensued and evolved regarding women's ordination to priesthood in The Episcopal Church and the Anglican Communion over a period of forty years.

The story told by the sixteen authors who in this volume reflect on this pivotal event both personally and theologically help to define where both The Episcopal Church and the Communion of which it is a part have both evolved and have failed to do so over these four decades.

Significant to me concerning that day, in addition to the event itself, are the words spoken by the late Rev. Paul Matthews Washington, then rector of the Advocate, just prior to the start of the service, as he customarily stretched his upper torso over the small lectern at the front of the church's nave and with also customarily outstretched hands laid out for the nearly two thousand persons assembled the significance of what was about to take place.

He quietly said: "Good Christian people: in response to and in obedience to God the Holy Spirit, we the Church—baptized,

---

1 Thanks to the generosity of Bishop Barbara C. Harris and the editors of *Anglican & Episcopal History* for sharing this introductory foreword which also appears in that journal, cf. vol. 83, no. 2 (Summer 2014).

confirmed, ordained, and consecrated members of Christ's Body—have come together from all over this land and beyond, to ordain to the sacred order of the priesthood persons commended by you, admitted to the order of deacons, and found qualified to be ordained priests by the bishops who will ordain them.

"Our actions today are untimely, but the dilemma is what is one to do when the democratic process, the political dynamics, and the legal guidelines are out of step with the imperative which says: 'Now is the time!' and 'What is a mother to do when the doctor says, "Your baby will be born on August 10th," when on July 29th she has reached the last stages of labor and the water sack has ruptured?'"

He concluded by saying; "May we see in this day which is upon us a day which the Lord has made. May we rejoice and be glad in it. May we accept the rightness of this action as a call above its timing. May we accept the justice in this action as a call outweighing technicalities. May we accept the spirit as life, knowing that the letter killeth. May we praise the Lord for those this day who act in obedience to God, as we love and respect those this day whom we cannot obey."[2]

When his remarks were followed by the opening hymn, "Come, Labor On," the huge congregation gathered for the service erupted in laughter.

Reaction to the Philadelphia ordinations, particularly that of bishops of the church, including the presiding bishop, was swift and vehement. It included a hastily called emergency meeting of the House of Bishops and continued to be argued at the subsequent regularly scheduled meeting of the House later in the year. I also recall a specially called meeting of the church's Executive Council in New York City. The bishop of Louisiana, a member of that Council, was killed in the crash of a commercial airline flight en route to that meeting. The bishop of another diocese blamed the Philadelphia ordinands for his death, saying, in effect, that had they not done what they did, the bishop would not have been on the ill-fated flight. In response to that pronouncement, I sent him a telegram strongly suggesting that, given his un-Christian remarks, he consider returning his baptismal certificate. A second irregular ordination service that

---

2   *"Other Sheep I Have": The Autobiography of Father Paul M. Washington* (Philadelphia: Temple University Press, 1994), 168.

took place in Washington, DC, the following year similarly drew the ire of the bishops, and statements decrying both actions ensued.

The General Convention of 1976, perhaps encouraged by approval of women's ordination by the Anglican Church of Canada, and after lengthy and rancorous debate, along with fervent prayer in both the House of Bishops and the House of Deputies—comprised of both clergy and laity—made the necessary canonical change or amendment to church law that would make participation in all orders of ministry—deacons, priests, and bishops—applicable to women and men.

There was, of course, wide mixed reaction among those attending the convention, both as voting members and visitors. While many applauded the decision, I recall a rather rotund priest sitting on a street curb dissolved in tears, lamenting aloud the injury the change made to all his images of the Anglican fathers. "Besides," he asked, choking back tears, "what would a pregnant priest look like?" To which the woman accompanying me replied: "About like you." An uncertain interim period ensued in which some interesting things took place, including celebrations of the Eucharist by some of the Philadelphia Eleven.

Regular ordination began with the Rev. Jackie Means on January 1, 1977, followed by others in the years immediately following. The initial slow pace will, no doubt, be examined by some of the authors of this volume as well as what those initial years entailed. Equal access to priestly ordination did not in and of itself guarantee equal access to exercise of priestly ministry. For several years women priests, in many instances, while not by fiat but practice, found themselves somewhat limited and restricted in their calls and employment, even as their experience increased.

Subsequent years saw large numbers of women's ordination. Unfortunately to this day, and to my knowledge, there is no accurate count of those priested either living or deceased. Positions for women clergy did, however, continue to increase both quantitatively and qualitatively. Women were called as rectors, some to large congregations known as "cardinal parishes," and their priests dubiously called "cardinal rectors." Some became deans of cathedrals, others canons on diocesan staff, institutional chaplains, and members of divinity school faculties. Three have been named deans and presidents of seminaries, two of whom continue to serve.

The emergence of LGBT (Lesbian, Gay, Bisexual, and Trans-gendered persons) concerns, in the ordination process and in other areas of the life of the church, are in and of themselves also subjects worthy of examination in this volume. Certainly we have seen the ordination of fellow Christians in these self-identified sexual orientations, including the consecrations of an openly gay partnered, and subsequently an out partnered lesbian as bishops of the church.

The decision to make the ordination process equally available to women meant, of course, the election and consecration of women bishops. At this writing the church has seen this inevitability result in the election, consecration, and exercise of that office by twenty women since 1989 and the election of a woman as presiding bishop and primate in 2006 in this province of the Communion alone. One is deceased and six are retired. A few of the latter group continue some limited exercise of the office.

One of the unfortunate aspects of the emergence of women bishops has been the fact that not enough women allow their names to go forward in the Episcopal election process. If, indeed more would do so, that overall number could perhaps markedly increase.

Twenty years after 1974, Dr. Pamela W. Darling, then a lecturer in church history, episcopal polity, and women's issues at General Theological Seminary in New York City and Lutheran Theological Seminary in Philadelphia, wrote a volume *New Wine: The Story of Women Transforming Leadership and Power in the Episcopal Church*. She also served as the special assistant to the first woman president of the General Convention's House of Deputies and as a consultant to the then Committee on the Status of Women.

In the conclusion of that volume Dr. Darling wrote:

> The bursting of old wineskins is messy and painful, but as we discover the nature of the new wine, we will be able to fashion suitable new containers. In an odd way, traditionalists and feminists may inadvertently work together to educate the rest of the church, so that future decisions arise out of a consistent view of human nature, personal relationships, and social organization—created, judged, saved, and empowered by the one triune God.[3]

---

3 Pamela W. Darling, *New Wine: The Story of Women Transforming Leadership and Power in the Episcopal Church* (Cambridge, MA: Cowley Publications: 1994), 231.

Indeed, forty years ago the old wineskins began to burst as an irregular ordination service unfolded at an inner city church in Philadelphia. You are invited to enjoy the unfolding of this story through the "voices" of the authors who have contributed to this book.

Forty years later, there are women priests in nearly every province of the Anglican Communion, and several provinces have seen the election and selection of woman bishops including New Zealand, Canada, Cuba, Australia, Southern Africa, and most recently, the Church of South India.

While the year 2014 marks the fortieth anniversary of women to priesthood in The Episcopal Church and twenty-five years of women as bishops to the episcopate, it marks much more than that. It is in some ways a culmination of more than a hundred years of women's struggle of full inclusion in a church for which they raised and gave money to erect and maintain buildings large and small, basically supported male clergy, established and maintained missionary efforts at home and abroad, and established educational and social justice programs for the emancipation of women throughout the world.

The chapters of this volume will document that history and reflect on what we have learned theologically, socially, communally, and practically from this first experience and now commonly accepted practice.

As mentioned earlier there is no accurate published record of the number of ordained women, despite their inclusion in clergy directories. My concern however, goes beyond actual numbers and has more to do with what we have or have not learned over these many years. While I am gratified that we have reached this forty-year milestone, I am not sure we have reached any maturity in the reality of this living witness and phenomenon.

The Rt. Reverend Barbara C. Harris
Bishop Suffragan, Massachusetts (Retired)

INTRODUCTION

Getting a Running Start on the Future

Can you see it? There is a wide smile on my face as I write this introduction. I have been trying to catch up and catch on to women's religious history for almost fifty years. The short story is that in 1965 I told my PhD dissertation advisers that I wished to write on women's religious history. Their responses came quickly: "No!" "Way too trendy." "You'll never get a job in a *real* history department." My favorite quip was, "There simply is not enough data!"

Temporarily stymied, I demurred and promptly wrote on popular responses to the English Reformation . . . including men and, of course, women. In one way or another I have been happily writing about women and chasing down their historical experiences ever since. Along the way, I also acquired a taste for understanding popular responses to groundbreaking events.

The blunt fact is that my over forty years of professional experience—as teacher, administrator, and leader of efforts to support theological education in Episcopal seminaries—coincides aptly with the era that is the focus of this volume. About the same time that I was seeking to exercise my vocation as a professor of church history, my denominational sisters were increasingly seeking ordination to all three orders of ministry. Our "herstories," our times, our ties are vocationally and formationally intertwined.

As a young feminist I learned daily that the personal is political. The hard, and at times humorous, challenges I faced as the sole woman on a seminary faculty and the struggles for women's ordination in The Episcopal Church were signs of the times. Our personal stories were firmly shaped amid the significant political legacies of the civil rights movement, the battle for the ERA (Equal Rights Amendment), the War on Poverty, and the first and second waves of feminism. These bold engagements over fifty years ago clearly crossed bridges built by women and their supporters in much earlier decades.

The broad story of women's diverse and persistently engaged contributions to American religion now has encyclopedic chroniclers. In the nineteenth century the words and wisdom of women often shaped denominational realities. Episcopal women led efforts at renewal and reform, emphasized education and social service, participated and led in funding domestic and foreign mission.[1] Just when does the story for women's leadership start? With Eve, as one author suggests? With more focused vision, when do we begin to tell the story of women's struggle for ordered and episcopally-sanctioned service?[2] In 1855 with a bishop of Maryland who sets apart two deaconesses? What about the significant history of deaconesses' service from the 1880s onward, despite the fact that the Church Pension Fund in 1919 insisted deaconesses were not clergy? Certainly the 1944 ordination to the Anglican priesthood of Florence Li Tim-Oi in Hong Kong by Bishop Hall is significant; as is Bishop James Pike's 1965 recognition of Deaconess Phyllis Edwards as a deacon, thereby enabling her to be entitled "The Rev." Or should I as a lay reader today pay more attention to the 1925 action by the House of Deputies to license women as lay readers, a proposal rejected by the House of Bishops? By the way, it was not until 1969 that women were "authorized" as lay readers and chalice bearers. This decision was followed a year later

---

1 See Rosemary Ruether and Rosemary Keller, eds., *Encyclopedia of Women in Religion in America* (Bloomington: Indiana University Press, 2005) and in particular, Fredrica Harris Thompsett, "Women in the American Episcopal Church," I, 269–79. For further information, see Mary S. Donovan, *A Different Call: Women's Ministries in the Episcopal Church, 1825–1920* (Wilton, CT: Morehouse Barlow, 1986) and Sheryl A. Kujawa-Holbrook, ed., *Freedom Is a Dream: A Documentary History of Episcopal Women* (New York: Church Publishing, 2002). Mention should also be made of the work of the Episcopal Women's History Project (EWHP), which since 1980 has in several venues fostered and encouraged knowledge of women's history.

2 The now classic text for evaluating women's leadership is Pamela W. Darling, *New Wine: The Story of Women Transforming Leadership and Power in the Episcopal Church* (Cambridge, MA: Cowley Publications, 1991). I am further indebted to Pam for gathering chronological data. I am even more gratified that she agreed to write an opening chapter for this present volume.

by women's admission as deputies to General Convention, an action also marked by a fifty-year struggle.

At this point I must pause. I know that my prophetic mentor and theological champion of the laity, Verna Dozier, would mutter and insist that our primary focus should be on the whole people of God. To tell the truth, we have only begun to chronicle the opportunities and vocational histories pursued by laywomen and laymen.[3] While the focus of *Looking Forward, Looking Backward* is occasioned by a specific event, the stories and accounts in each chapter are shaped and offered in behalf of the whole people of God.

I first imagined and passionately shaped this volume a year ago with a sense of urgency. Yes, it would take speed not only to design, but also to publish a volume by the time of the fortieth anniversary of the July 1974 Philadelphia ordinations. I wished to honor the courageous leadership of my Philadelphia and Washington sisters and their brotherly companions. I desired to express this gratitude with the fullness of academic scholarship and contemporary voices. I also know, from working with younger seminarians, that many today are unaware of hard-fought legacies and accompanying power dynamics that still have an effect on our future. I am committed and resolved to learn from the consequences that these pioneers inspired and we are left to pursue. Moreover, I do not want to let this opportune time for critical reflection pass by without substantial historical, theological, and pastoral reflection.

I am particularly thankful for early encouragement and wisdom from Gay Clark Jennings and Rebecca Wilson in shaping this volume. All along the way Nancy Bryan, editorial director of Church Publishing, has offered friendship, enthusiasm, and expertise. To each of the authors who just a few months ago said "yes" to my invitation and then responded with splendid contributions, my gratitude remains unbounded.

Just what have we learned? Where are we now? Where have we failed? What have we yet to do? One of my favorite mentors, the historian of American religion, Martin Marty, once noted, "We study history in order to intervene in history." In this mandated time for revisioning our church's mission and future, just what interventions

---

3 In addition to the texts cited above, see Fredrica Harris Thompsett and Sheryl A. Kujawa-Holbrook, *Deeper Joy: Lay Women and Vocation in the 20th Century Episcopal Church* (New York: Church Publishing, 2005).

are we called to make? This focus requires more than historical and demographic consequences; it formidably carries ethical and theological imperatives, as well as ecclesiological and liturgical emphases. Certainly as one contributor persuasively observes, "the strong doctrine of baptism . . . bears repeating" again and again. In the past month as I have traveled amid Boston's large Roman Catholic presence, I have seen both a button and a bumper sticker that read: "If you're not going to ordain women, stop baptizing them!"[4] We used these same words in the 1970s. Today I continue to savor the theological clarity of this maxim! I am reminded as well that our actions and words offer encouragement to others. As I have become more deeply aware of the Spirit-saturated waters of Holy Baptism, I realize that I do not need further approval to engage in God's mission. We are all theologians, students of God's word and ways. Further, I believe we have all the permission we need, an authority grounded in the goodness of creation, recognized in baptism, and nourished amid compassionate, justice-seeking communities.

The subject of this book invites deeper reflection on more liberating understandings of what it is to be human. Postmodern analysis and scholarship, in particular from younger authors, point to the complexities of our lives and identities. T. S. Eliot in *Four Quartets* acclaimed the use of memory for human freedom—"liberation from the future as well as the past." It is indeed appropriate that Presiding Bishop Katharine Jefferts Schori concludes this volume with expansive biblical and contemporary vision. Calling for the care of the whole creation, she advocates a different future, one with "adequate food, community healing, and justice for all."

I have long believed that one reason we study the past is to get a running start on the future. I am persuaded that we can convert understanding of past events into insights that will illumine our future. Please join me as we learn from and with the assembled host of talented authors, scholars, pastors, storytellers, and leaders who have contributed to this volume. They have sobering, at times amusing, often challenging, and deeply instructive lessons to share. We each and all have work yet to do as we pursue the gospel of

---

4 This axiom appears today on the website of the Women's Ordination Conference: A Voice for Women in the Catholic Church: http://www.womensordination.org/content/view/242/ (accessed January 2, 2014).

transformation. Emboldened by lessons that we have learned, let us move forward to celebrate the fortieth anniversary of women to the priesthood with smiles upon our faces.

Fredrica Harris Thompsett
Cambridge and Cape Cod

FREDRICA HARRIS THOMPSETT has been a seminary professor, author, and scholar of Anglican history and theology for the past forty years. Her current (and overlong) title is Mary Wolfe Professor Emerita of Historical Theology at the Episcopal Divinity School (EDS) in Cambridge, Massachusetts. Her most recent books are *Born of Water, Born of Spirit: Supporting the Ministry of the Baptized in Small Congregations,* coauthored with Sheryl Kujawa-Holbrook (Herndon, VA: Alban Institute, 2010); and an edited volume, *Encouraging Conversation: Resources for Talking about Same-Sex Blessings* (New York: Morehouse Publishing, 2013). A current member of The Episcopal Church's Executive Council, she is a lively speaker, an occasional preacher, and an enthusiastic advocate of the ministries of clergy and laity alike.

CHAPTER 1

Forty Years On—Notes on Priesthood, Women, and The Episcopal Church

Pamela W. Darling

From our vantage point in the twenty-first century, it appears inevitable that women would join men in all orders of ministry in The Episcopal Church. But for centuries, ordaining women to the priesthood was virtually unthinkable. In the late 1960s, a student from a non-Episcopal seminary wore a seminarian's collar with the black stripe while visiting the Episcopal convent where I was a novice. I confess I was among the wide-eyed who giggled at what was surely a joke. As it has turned out, the joke was on me: the person in a striped collar in 1967 is today a priest and a senior member of that order of nuns, regularly celebrating the Eucharist in the convent chapel. The unthinkable has become routine.

My generation of "decently and in order" Episcopalians, who had to overcome shock at the very idea, is passing away. Our personal paths to acceptance varied dramatically: short or lengthy, easy or traumatic, on a timetable independent of official actions of the General Convention, or of the ecclesiastical disobedience of a few pioneers. Although the ordination of the "Philadelphia 11" caused consternation and outrage among the "establishment" (especially among bishops), it thrilled and gave hope to many, hope that has proven well-founded. It is sometimes difficult to recall how intense the conflict seemed at the time, or even to remember why.

1

Where Are They Now?

In the decades since, attitudes and expectations in most corners of The Episcopal Church have changed dramatically. For one thing, there are the sheer numbers. In 1980, it was possible to recognize and know by name every woman priest. By 2013, 4,564 women had been ordained to the priesthood—37.8 percent of the total 12,086 ordained since 1976. In addition, 59 percent of deacons ordained during that period were women, 1,867 out of a total 3,167.[1] The gender ratio of graduating seminarians seems likely to increase the proportion of women in the priesthood even more. Today it would be unusual to find an Episcopalian who had never encountered a "woman priest."

Women now minister in a wide variety of roles within the traditional structures of parish and diocese—interims and rectors of parishes, from small to large, multistaffed congregations; deans of cathedrals and seminaries; divinity school and seminary faculty; canons of dioceses and cathedrals; members of boards and commissions; bishops, both suffragan and diocesan. By 2006, in the House of Bishops outrage had been replaced by admiration: they elected a woman as presiding bishop.

Some ordained women moved beyond parochial/diocesan boxes, which had been none too welcoming to women in the early years. Chaplaincies in hospitals, schools, seaports, and nursing homes were more accessible (and more likely to provide a living wage). Others launched out further, establishing spiritual centers and retreat houses, or creating programs and congregations of the hungry and the homeless, single mothers, street people, addicts, prostitutes, and others of the sort Jesus commended to our care.

Who Are They Now?

"Women priests" today come in all shapes and sizes, liturgical and sartorial styles, personality types and spiritual traditions, preaching skills and political acumen, leadership traits and pastoral abilities—just like male priests (though women probably have more sartorial options). Most are happy to love even the smallest congregation,

---

1 Data provided in October 2013 by the Church Pension Group, courtesy of Mark Duffy of the Archives of the Episcopal Church. These figures do not include the sixteen women "irregularly" ordained priest in 1974 and 1975.

despite the typical part-time pay. More than one failing parish has been loved back into self-respect and self-sufficiency by a woman. In small churches and large cathedrals, they have emphasized hands-on outreach to the surrounding community—food pantries, urban gardens, tutoring programs, language classes. Yes, male priests do that too, and most of the "hands" have belonged to laywomen; but ordained women are particularly good cheerleaders when a congregation dares to do something new.

Despite a lack of evidence, from time to time fear arises that women in leadership will somehow drive men away. Worry about gender imbalance has increased in every period of significant ecclesiastical change, in part because changing the gender balance destabilizes power structures within a congregation or diocese. Women tend to exercise leadership differently than men, who benefit from the authority automatically ascribed to them by the culture. Theoretically, absence of a male leader could be experienced as absence of leadership altogether, which can make parishioners feel insecure enough to leave. But in fact, a 2003 survey found that "neither men nor women perceive a significant difference in church membership trends between churches with ordained women on staff and those without."[2]

Reams of anecdotal evidence suggest that the ordination process has tended to favor men over women, as have search and deployment patterns, in some dioceses more than others. But year by year discrimination in these areas declines, as bishops, commissions on ministry and deployment officers recognize the gifts women bring to the ordained ministry—and as more bishops, deployment officers, and members of ministry commissions are themselves ordained women.

The Dark Side

Problems remain. Some women burn out quickly, or leave active ministry—for any number of reasons. Some believed the church would change faster, or slower, and were worn down by continual disappointment. Some tried to emulate a beloved (male) rector and were disillusioned to find that people did not respond to her as they

---

2 "Reaching Toward Wholeness II," a survey presented to the General Convention in 2003 by the Executive Council Committee on the Status of Women.

had to him. Some came through the process and were ordained after it was no longer controversial, and were stunned to discover that the church is still home to misogyny. For them it hadn't been an issue, but protesting "I'm not a feminist!" did not prepare them for being slighted and discounted in myriad small and large ways. Discrimination or harassment illegal in the secular workplace flourished in some dioceses.

In the early years (I devoutly hope it is no longer true), some newly-ordained women were stunned by vulgar insinuations and propositions from male clergy, including bishops. Ordained women teased apart the intricate connections between gender roles, sexuality, and clericalism. They violated the old-boy code of secrecy, exposing clerical abuse that had previously been tolerated and protected. Others tried to be "just one of the boys," but that camaraderie stopped at the restroom door. I love the story about Bishop Barbara Harris, who certainly never aspired to be "one of the boys." During a break in the House of Bishops meeting soon after she became the first woman bishop in the Anglican Communion, she joined several other bishops in strategizing about an issue soon coming to a vote. The group drifted toward the back of the room, and the other bishops, still in lively conversation, all disappeared into the men's room. Bishop Harris, the story goes, didn't hesitate. Pushing the door slightly open, she called out, "If you don't stop talking about that right now, I'm coming in."

Outside the Episcopal Bubble

None of these things occurred in a cultural vacuum. Indeed, most Episcopalians were immersed in the social ferment of the 1950s, 60s, and 70s—the movements for civil rights, women's liberation, and gay pride which challenged power structures and turned conventional attitudes upside down—along with the international religious renewal sparked by Pope John XXIII and the Second Vatican Council.

There was resistance, in and outside the church. Were we selling out to the godless spirit of the age, or daring to follow the Spirit into a new era? The conflict was acute, to the point that some left The Episcopal Church, charging the church had actually left them by embracing dangerous beliefs and practices. Relationships were damaged or broken. There was much grief and anger, as those holding to a male-only priesthood created new institutional structures to protect that fundamental principle.

For the rest, clergy, people, and congregations adapted to an ongoing process of ecclesial transformation, just as organizations and people outside the church were adapting to changing societal norms affecting race and gender, power and leadership. Women entered shop floors and boardrooms, courtrooms and stock exchanges, the sanctums of government from city hall to the Congress of the United States. Some days it seems a painfully slow transformation, but looking back forty or fifty years reveals an extraordinary range, not just of "first women" invading male sanctums, but of changed expectations symbolized by the cliché that a girl child today can aspire to being a bishop or the president.

What Difference Does It Make?

Thirty years ago, psychologist Carol Gilligan offered a gender-based theory of difference between women's "ethic of care" and men's "ethic of justice."[3] Her work, with its alternate perspective on moral development and the value of a distinctive female voice, was a foundational contribution to the ongoing discussion about the "equality" of the sexes. Does "equal" mean "same"? Are differences between men and women biologically based? Are they social constructions? Are they imaginary? Do women inhabit the priestly role differently than men? Do they lead in different ways? Do they bring special gifts to the ordained ministry?

For most of Christian history, so far as we can tell, priesthood was a male enterprise. The authority of the priest was intertwined with the authority of the male in secular society. Leadership and pastoral styles were shaped by masculine characteristics and values. They are not easy to separate, but the lived priestly experience of thousands of women is demonstrating that authentic priesthood can be exercised by women, bringing a new experience of wholeness to the body of Christ.

I'd love to know what it will all look like forty years from now.

---

3 Carol Gilligan, *In a Different Voice: Psychological Theory and Women's Development* (Cambridge, MA: Harvard University Press, 1982).

PAMELA W. DARLING is retired from a lifetime as a "professional Episco-palian"—novice in the Order of St Helena; fellow at General Theological Seminary, where she earned a doctorate in church history; consultant and writer for numerous church organizations and committees; a decade of service as assistant to Pamela P. Chinnis, the first woman to serve as president of the House of Deputies of the General Convention; author of *New Wine: The Story of Women Transforming Leadership and Power in the Episcopal Church* (Cowley, 1994). In her current incarnation, as volunteer in the Neonatal Intensive Care Unit of the local hospital holding babies withdrawing from drugs to which they were exposed in utero, she is dis-covering that the face of Christ can be found in squalling infants, their frightened mothers, and the awesome NICU nurses.

CHAPTER 2

Feminization of the Clergy and the Future: Sociological Reflections

Paula D. Nesbitt

"Women opened the door to the priesthood forty years ago; I assumed that gender equality would be the norm by now," a young female priest recently told me. Her remarks echo those of other young women who have watched the careers of male seminary colleagues move up a glass escalator while theirs have seemed to plateau. For some women, the shock, disappointment, and frustration of becoming aware that gender inequalities still persist in the church sets apart a generation of women who expected better. Many assumed that the sacrifices made by women four decades earlier had resolved the gender issue.

The Philadelphia Eleven changed history by undertaking an act that would ultimately hasten women's ordination to the priesthood in the church overall. Today women make up nearly half of those annually ordained to the priesthood, and about one-third of all active priests.[1] At least 15 percent of the church's 110 dioceses have experienced women as diocesan, suffragan, or provisional bishops. Ordained women currently hold the two highest leadership offices in the church: presiding bishop and president of the House of Deputies. Yet this tremendous

---

1 Anne L. Hurst, Kyle E. Walker, Derek Y. Darves-Bornoz, Susan T. Erdey, and Matthew J. Price, *The State of the Clergy 2012: A Report for The Episcopal Church* (New York: Office of Research, Church Pension Group, 2012).

breakthrough can overshadow the challenges that remain, rendering persisting gender inequalities more difficult to see and voice.

Feminization of the Priesthood Revisited

The priesthood like law, medicine, and other professions has been feminized in terms of the rising percentage of women who have entered since the 1970s. In secular occupations, feminization has been linked to other traits such as declining prestige, fewer young men seeking to enter, and decreasing compensation when compared to nonfeminized occupations. Additionally, women become clustered into certain types of positions within feminized occupations, often at lower levels while the fewer young men who enter tend to be fast-tracked on a *glass escalator*[2] to management positions offering leadership and higher compensation. Feminization as a result often has been blamed for damaging an occupation. Never has it been heralded as a positive trend.

Nearly two decades ago in a study of Episcopal clergy,[3] I showed how some of the trends linked with feminization actually began prior to women's ordination. By the early 1970s, church membership was eroding from its peak little more than a decade earlier, budgets were tightening, controversies and conflict were endemic within the church over a range of issues such as the role of public activism, prayer book revision, and women's ordination. Both the number and average age of men entering the priesthood were rising, which created a growing pool of clergy for relatively fewer full-time and leadership positions than a decade earlier. Secular professions and opportunities also continued to poach the priesthood in terms of pastoral roles, responsibilities, and prestige while occupational self-understanding shifted from being set apart for ministry to enabling the ministry of all.[4]

The fresh visibility of female clergy during a period when full-time placements, budgets, and membership were eroding, as well as

---

2 Christine Williams, "The Glass Escalator: Hidden Advantages for Men in the 'Female' Professions," *Social Problems* 39, no. 3 (1992): 253–67.

3 Paula D. Nesbitt, *Feminization of the Clergy in America: Occupational and Organizational Perspectives* (New York: Oxford University Press, 1997).

4 For instance, pastoral care and counseling have become differentiated, with the latter normally requiring an advanced secular degree as a path to licensing. Also see Nesbitt, *Feminization of the Clergy in America*, 100–05, 152–54; and Sherryl Kleinman, *Equals Before God: Seminarians as Humanistic Professionals* (Chicago: University of Chicago Press, 1984), 4–11, 24–27.

a growing sense that men no longer would own the priesthood, triggered assumptions that women's ordination and occupational feminization were the cause of the changes occurring. By the late 1980s, a subtle backlash against women's ordination had begun to slow the strides being made toward gender parity. The backlash included nostalgic assumptions that the priesthood had lost the best and the brightest clergy as well as undermining talented female clergy through subtle attributions that they seemed a bit angry or aggressive, or questioning their ability or qualifications for leadership positions. Furthermore, as the vocational diaconate concurrently grew and feminized, some women reported pressure from their diocese to consider that vocational role instead of priesthood. During this time, the fewer young men being ordained moved more quickly into rectorships and leadership positions than did male clergy over the previous decade, while female priests were more likely to move laterally into staff positions and part-time placements.[5]

A series of accommodating changes that overwhelmingly affected female clergy such as conscience clauses, flying bishops and alternative pastoral care arrangements, and prohibitions in some dioceses against interims being called as rector, served to limit women's opportunity and authority even though their competency in the priesthood and then the episcopate was both demonstrated and officially accepted. In short, the willingness to help women break fresh occupational ground was counterbalanced by anxieties over changing tradition, culture, and male dominance.

Gender parity or paradox?

After forty years of women in the priesthood, what strides have actually been made toward gender parity? Nearly a generation ago, my feminization study showed a persistent gender gap of nearly 20 percent in priests who had ever held a position as vicar or solo rector of a parish.[6] In the 2009 "Called to Serve" study,[7] the gender gap persists.

---

5   Nesbitt, *Feminization of the Clergy in* America, 58–59, 76–77, 82–83, 124–26.
6   Nesbitt, *Feminization of the Clergy in America*, 76–77.
7   The Executive Council's Committee on the Status of Women, The Church Pension Fund's Office of Research, The Episcopal Church Center's Office of Women's Ministry, CREDO Institute, *Called to Serve: A Study of Clergy Careers, Clergy Wellness, and Clergy Women. Preliminary Report* (New York: Church Pension Group, 2011), 16.

Across the four decades of women's ordination, two interesting trends appear (Figure 1). First, although the gender gap is widest among those ordained in the 1970s, it narrows and then widens again for priests ordained since 2000. Second, the percentage of priests ever holding rector or vicar positions has declined—among men as well as women.

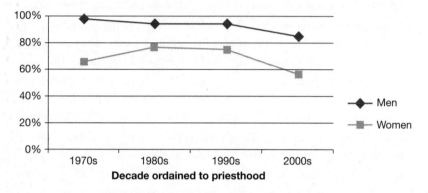

Figure 1. Percentage of Episcopal priests ever holding a rector or vicarship
Source: "Called to Serve" study, 2009

These trends suggest multiple possible causes, such as men being called to rector or vicar positions more often than women in recent years, women being less likely to apply for them, fewer rector and vicar positions available for the pool of active priests, or newer priests expressing their ministry in more varied ways. Although some have argued that women may have different aspirations than climbing the priesthood's traditional career ladder, the "Called to Serve" study found that young women today are about 25 percent more likely than men to have applied for such positions but not been called. Moreover, women continue to be significantly overrepresented in parish associate and other staff positions (51 percent) and underrepresented as senior clergy (19 percent), according to 2012 Church Pension Fund data.[8]

Another way to look at gender is by what women and men earn in their church ministry, which also affects what they likely will earn in the future and eventually their pension. In 2012, the *Church Compensation Report* showed that women continue to average only about 86 cents for every dollar that men earn.[9] Although the gender gap narrows a bit by the type of position that clergy hold, it never

---

8 Matthew J. Price and Anne Hurst, *The 2012 Church Compensation Report* (New York.: Church Pension Fund, 2013), 4.
9 Price and Hurst, *2012 Church Compensation Report*, 4.

disappears: Even among full-time parish associates and staff, women earn only 93 cents for every dollar paid to men. Nor does it disappear among clergy under age thirty-five, or by region (province) except in two cases: among associates in Province V and solo clergy in Province VI. The "Called to Serve" study also found that men were more likely than women to have successfully negotiated more compensation than originally offered, which affects the gender gap as well as earnings across the career. This raises questions for further research: How effectively are women negotiating? Or are those making an offer receptive to the same negotiation bid by women as by men?

Because of the legacy of racial discrimination, it is important to ask how race/ethnicity affects these trends in The Episcopal Church where clergy are about 95 percent Caucasian.[10] In my feminization study, while Caucasian men were overrepresented in senior-level positions, African-American women were overrepresented among women in senior leadership.[11] More recently, Church Pension Fund compensation data show that African-American male and female clergy tend to earn more than their Caucasian and Hispanic colleagues (Figure 2), suggesting good opportunities across racial differences. Yet the gender gap persists *within* each racial group, being the largest among Caucasian clergy (18 percent).

Paradoxically, the careers of female clergy are still more likely than those of men to include a "second shift" of personal care-giving

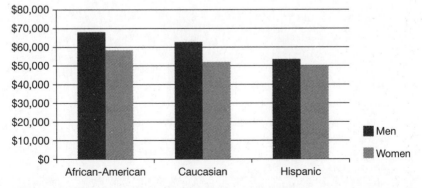

Figure 2. Median compensation for clergy by gender and racial/ethnic group
Source: The State of the Clergy 2006, Church Pension Group

---

10 Racial/ethnic data are estimates. See Matthew J. Price, *The State of the Clergy 2006* (New York: Church Pension Group, 2006), 14–15 including notes and text.
11 Nesbitt, *Feminization of the Clergy in America*, 86.

and other forms of work involved with managing household and family life.[12] Although men participate more in household and family tasks than two generations ago, women are still responsible for a greater share of the work in heterosexual households, according to the "Called to Serve" study. This can limit the placements that women are able to hold, as well as their ability to seek positions that require a long commute or a move to another region. Nonetheless, women in their twenties and thirties were still more likely than men their age to have applied but not been called to solo-clergy placements. Women have reported being asked questions by parish search committees about childcare and other matters not asked of men, which would be discriminatory in secular settings.

While being single can allow more opportunity for women to pursue their careers, there can be trade-offs. The "Called to Serve" study found that marriage enhanced men's careers but had a penalty effect for women, similar to findings in secular occupations. At the same time, single male priests viewed their ordination as an asset to their social life, but women viewed it the opposite way, which points to a double bind that women face: whether they are married or single, they face liabilities in their ordained career in ways that men do not.

At the conclusion of my 1990s study, I wrote, "The future of women clergy realistically appears to be one increasingly crowded with female colleagues in lower to mid-level placements as the occupation continues to feminize."[13] Although recent data show more women integrating into solo clergy and rectorships, some evidence points to them clustered more often in parishes with smaller membership and fewer resources, and perhaps less than full-time compensation. Furthermore, in 2012, only about half as many women as men working full-time held senior-level positions (such as a rectorship with paid clergy staff, cathedral dean, full seminary professor or dean, or bishop).[14] As a result, women may be integrating more fully into midlevel positions but sizable gender gaps still remain in compensation and attainment.

---

12 Arlie Russell Hochschild's book *The Second Shift* (New York: Penguin, 2003) has resulted in the term's widespread use in gender and work studies; see p. 7 for how the term is used. Also see The Executive Council's Committee on the Status of Women, The Church Pension Fund's Office of Research, The Episcopal Church Center's Office of Women's Ministry, CREDO Institute, *Called to Serve*, 5.
13 Nesbitt, *Feminization of the Clergy in America*, 164.
14 See Price and Hurst, *2012 Church Compensation Report*, 4. Based on the percentage of women to clergy overall, women represented only 55 percent of what would be the expected number of women in senior positions.

Stained-Glass Ceiling for Women or Not?

The phrase "glass ceiling" has been used for more than two decades to suggest invisible barriers for women's careers in senior and executive leadership. Its invisibility suggests that what may need to change can be difficult to identify, unlike two generations ago where barriers were quite visible. Since then, women have moved into the highest levels of church leadership and opened up imaginative possibilities for other women. To what extent is the "stained-glass ceiling" a valid metaphor anymore?

Men are still more likely to apply and to be called or elected to senior leadership positions, according to the "Called to Serve" data, even when neutralizing the effects of age and year of ordination, past or present ability to be geographically mobile, and other factors. The most challenging trend is the disparity between the number of women who have been finalists in bishop search processes and the number elected. An increasing number of dioceses have named women as finalist nominees, but they are not any more likely to be elected than nearly two decades ago. By 2013, only three (2.7 percent) of the church's 110 diocesan bishops were female. Moreover, all female diocesan bishops who have retired or left office have been replaced by men.

The slow pace of women's integration into senior leadership suggests that either they are encountering active resistance or simply the gender-segregated culture has not changed sufficiently to allow women access to church leadership in more than token numbers. This supports the notion of a glass ceiling despite the visibility of women at the highest leadership level. Moreover, the few female senior leaders can become viewed as icons of achievement, symbolizing gender diversity in the ministry without threatening either cultural norms or men's prospects for senior leadership.[15] Their visibility also can draw attention away from patterns of gender inequity, making it more difficult to address. Some have claimed that the "gender problem" has been solved and that the church's attention to women's ministries or the status of women is no longer meaningful. Yet the few women at the top remain isolated, to some

---

15 Paula D. Nesbitt, "Clergy and Gender in US—American Sociology of Religion Research and Debate," in *Geschlechter-verhältnisse und Pfarrberuf im Wandel: Irritationen, Analysen und Forschungsperspektiven,* ed. Simone Mantei, Regina Sommer, and Ulrike Wagner-Rau, 149–64 (Stuttgart: Kohlhammer, 2013).

extent dependent upon the collegial good will of male colleagues and leaders, similar to patterns of tokenism that Kanter[16] identified in her classic corporate leadership study four decades ago.

Climbing through the cracks

Despite women still facing more challenges than men in their ministry, the data suggest steps that women interested in leadership might take. First, they must apply for leadership positions. In the "Called to Serve" study, women were less likely than men to have entered a search process for a senior leadership position such as cathedral dean or bishop, not counting those called or elected. This questions whether women may choose other paths for their ministry because of a clear vocational call or whether they hesitate because of gender-related concerns such as the lengthy history of women not being elected or called, conflict aggravated by gender bias, demands of "second shift" family care-giving, the stress of role expectations for leadership positions originally developed to fit male career patterns and interests, lack of encouragement by others, or perhaps an overdose of humility about their leadership potential. If so, what needs to change about church leadership that might attract more talented female clergy?

Second, women should try again despite the challenges. Women were less likely than men to consider entering another bishop search process in both "Called to Serve" and a study of bishop elections between 2002 and 2008,[17] indicating that the pool of female candidates for church leadership may be depleting faster than that of men. The elections study also found that women had considered the diocesan profile more carefully in their discernment to enter a search than did men, suggesting that they had entered searches where they could be a good fit. Women also were more likely than men to have been supported by their spouse or partner to enter the process, implying strong personal and family support for their career. However, women

---

16 Rosabeth Moss Kanter, *Men and Women of the Corporation* (New York: Basic Books, 1977).

17 See Paula D. Nesbitt with Judith A. Stark and William King, *Episcopal Transitions and Elections Survey Report 2009–10*, The Episcopal Church, The Office of Pastoral Development and the College for Bishops, 2010), 30; Paula Nesbitt, "Whatever Happened to the Glass Ceiling?" Paper presented at the Joint Meeting of the Scientific Study of Religion and the Religious Research Association, Baltimore, MD, 2010.

were overwhelmingly more likely to report gender as an issue during the process, especially once the nominees were presented to the electing diocese, which suggests that improvements could be made. Some women commented that they were willing to try again for the sake of other women, but that the emotional cost was very great.

Third, continuing education may be helpful for women interested in senior leadership. Women in secular occupations have benefitted from educational credentials as an objective sign of their expertise. The "Called to Serve" data also found that female bishops were more likely to have education beyond the MDiv degree than either female applicants or female priests overall. This pattern wasn't found among men, which suggests that education may be a distinctive asset for women's candidacy.

The study found other noteworthy differences. For instance, female bishops tended to see themselves as less liberal in both theology and on social issues than did female applicants, differing little from male bishops on average. Whether serving a diocese as bishop has a moderating effect on viewpoints or female bishops had been more moderate from the outset needs to be researched. Nonetheless, it does suggest the significance of a moderate perspective for church leadership today. Another disparity involved the greater likelihood of bishops—both female and male—to be either married or remarried, in contrast to female applicants and to priests overall. This may suggest a bias toward married clergy, which was supported by comments from single nominees on their visitation to an electing diocese. Since this study occurred before same-sex marriage was legal in some states, further research is needed on this topic.

GenX and Millennial Clergy

GenerationX and Millennial women have different assumptions and experiences of the ministry than women either ordained decades ago or entering more recently as a second career. The struggles for women's ordination and for changing structures and attitudes toward female clergy are a valued historical process that opened the doors of the priesthood and episcopate to women, but this history does not directly affect how they respond to actions or events as it often does for older women. While women directly shaped by second-wave feminism often had sought to integrate and transform aspects of the church that were dominated by male culture and power, younger generations have been less uncomfortable with tradition so long as there is both equal opportunity and personal relevance in whatever work they undertake.[18] In women's gatherings, generational tensions can emerge: younger women have little patience for the anger, cynicism, and sense of dominance that older women may display. They also want their voice, expressing a very different experience, to be heard.

The visibility of female priests and bishops during the latter twentieth century, as vocational models for girls and young women, has been beneficial. Figure 3 shows the age of women's first sense of call to the priesthood, which has declined rapidly from earlier generations to around age twenty, similar to men. Many younger women also went to seminary in an era of more supportive attitudes toward feminism in its various expressions, and had more female professors. And few were challenged or blocked in the ordination process because of their gender.

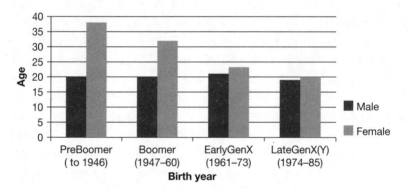

Figure 3. Gender and median age of first sense of call to priesthood
Source: "Called to Serve" study, 2009

Many young women have sought careers in parish ministry similar to those of their male seminary colleagues, but the data show an increasingly similar pattern to past decades as their ministry career paths unfold. Figure 4 points to a differing sense of opportunities in the ministry among young men and women today. While early GenX men and women felt an identical sense of opportunities, expressed by how easy it might be to find a suitable position in the church if

18 See Nesbitt, *Feminization of the Clergy in America, 171–72;* Joanna B. Gillespie, *Women Speak: Of God, Congregations and Change* (Valley Forge: Trinity Press International, 1995), 211–12.

needed, late GenX men are the most confident of all. Late GenX women are a little more confident than women born decades earlier.

Taken together, these trends suggest that young men, who have been underrepresented for decades, may be disproportionately rewarded for undertaking a ministry career. Young women evidently do not benefit in the same way from recruiting efforts and support for their ministry. Moreover, the gender gap is unlikely to close later in their careers. The "Called to Serve" study found that women were more likely than men to have seriously considered leaving the ministry altogether, and increasingly so among GenX women, which suggests a widespread frustration with their careers.

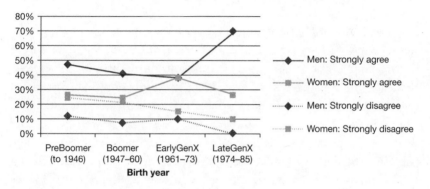

Figure 4. Ease of finding suitable paid Church position if needed
Source: "Called to Serve" study, 2009

Mentoring as a form of grooming future leaders through informal networks has been a powerful way of passing on valuable knowledge and recommending clergy for key opportunities in the ministry. Forty years ago, older clergy would identify promising young men and occasionally women with the ability and drive to break fresh ground in the church. Mentoring was effective but also exclusive, appreciated but not necessarily expected. Figure 5 shows how expectations for mentoring have changed, especially among GenX priests. The higher desire for mentoring among women may reflect a residual sense of a church's organizational culture and leadership structure still being largely male dominant. Yet the percentage of men and women who actually are mentored has been similar over the years. Although men continue as the largest source of mentors, young women are about 50 percent more likely than other women to have had mostly female mentors, which affirms inroads that women are making.

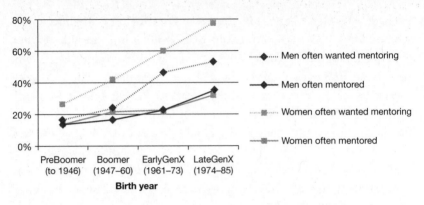

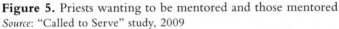

Figure 5. Priests wanting to be mentored and those mentored
Source: "Called to Serve" study, 2009

For Millennial and younger GenX female priests, women's ordination may feel somewhat like a stalled revolution. The altars have been opened, but career expectations seem more difficult to achieve. Instead, their paths point toward a hauntingly familiar pattern of gender disparity. The complex double bind in which women still find themselves—career penalties if married or single as well as "second shift" expectations—adds a level of stress that men seldom face. The situation of young women today not only needs more research but also demands action to not let gains toward gender parity in the church slip away through the illusion that gender no longer matters.

Moving Forward: Challenges and Opportunities for the Future

Concerns in the church today over the future of traditional full-time paid parish ministry and the need for more ministry models offers an opportunity to rethink ministry along with the tasks and expectations attached to it. Both women and men could benefit in future placements that model both wellness and gender-blind expectations. However any restructuring—in ministry or the church—must ask seriously how proposed changes will affect women as well as men, as well as the extent that they model wellness. Without such mindfulness, the gender trends among younger clergy suggest a future with a small core of largely men with full-time placements in prospering parishes, which position them for senior leadership, while everyone else scrambles to exercise their ordained ministry, perhaps serving multiple congregations, paid part-time, or in unpaid placements. Since these latter options may occur on top of secular work, such ministries likely will compete with personal and family care. Any two-tier priesthood may result in women having greater difficulty accumulating the experience and compensation necessary to contend for first-tier and leadership positions.

In the feminization study, I wrote about backlash or resistance to female clergy in the form of objectively changing rules, procedures, or structures with deliberate inattention to their potential disparate impact on women. Over the years such measures have continued, such as resolutions to limit the number of suffragan bishops in a diocese or to reduce the voice or vote of suffragan bishops churchwide, as well as eliminating ways by which gender can have an explicit voice in organizational development and change. New models of ministry and of church can present transformative opportunities for gender parity, but only if gender is part of the conversation. Tools such as gender monitoring, mainstreaming, and budgeting have had positive effects in other organizations, especially during periods of rapid change. The possibilities are profound for the future of women's ministry and leadership over the next forty years. Whichever direction they take will be a choice consciously and deliberately made.

PAULA D. NESBITT has studied gender and the Episcopal clergy for more than twenty-five years, starting with her doctoral research at Harvard (PhD, Sociology, 1990). Over the years she has published numerous articles and book chapters on gender and the clergy in addition to *Feminization of the Clergy in America* (Oxford University Press, 1997). She was a core research consultant for the 2009 "Called to Serve" and the 2009 Episcopal Transition and Elections studies cited in this chapter, as well as for other projects on gender and the clergy. Recently she led a cross-cultural research team for the Anglican Communion's Continuing Indaba and Mutual Listening Project, and evaluated the first women's indaba cosponsored with Anglican Women's Empowerment. She currently chairs the Executive Council's Committee on the Status of Women, on which she has served since 2009. Having taught for three seminaries and two universities, including ten years at the University of California, Berkeley, she currently is at the Graduate Theological Union. Ordained a priest for more than twenty years, she also is active in parish ministry.

CHAPTER 3

Liturgy and Worship—
Renewal of the Personal

Donald Schell

Through forty years of startling changes (and some upheaval and loss), women in ordained leadership contributed to healing our experience of church and human family. How? Obviously some stories point another direction—we've experienced schism and wounds. But despite many struggles, our congregations and church have found healing in experiencing women presiding at the Altar Table, and a renewal of ancient understanding of community and sacrament. Imperfectly, but perceptibly, and sometimes gracefully, we have come to celebrate the Eucharist as a gathering of particular diverse people who together make up one body in Christ. The human persons of our presiders have helped make that happen.

How has having ordained women in the pulpit and presiding at the Altar Table changed our experience? What first comes to mind is the noticing itself—we remember *particular* women (and men) and recall sensing in them something about *who* stands at the table and *how* we expect her or him to stand there. We have a more complex and specific personal experience of how different individuals speak and pray aloud, invite our voices of praise, embrace us at the peace, and offer holy things to the holy. Personal stories can help us see how this happened and what it means.

1.

Fifty years ago in a social economy that did not encourage women to ask vocational questions, my wife and I grew up a continent away. My wife's mother and my mother each found a way of presiding at the family meal that felt whole and authentic, but quite distinct. Was it West Coast vs. East Coast? Presbyterian vs. Episcopalian?

In my wife's house, her mother would cook dinner, put on a long, loose fitting dress, ready for her dad to come home from the bank and fix the two of them drinks. They'd watch the evening news and then Ellen's mother would call the older children to dinner. Once everyone was seated, her mother, at the head, would serve the meal.

In my house growing up, as my mother would finish cooking dinner, she'd get us children to set the table to be ready at 7 p.m., when my dad came home from office practice and hospital rounds. At precisely seven, we'd take our places and dad, at the head of the table, would say grace and serve the meal.

This was the era of *Leave it To Beaver*. Either house fits that sitcom's picture of order. Both women told their children that they'd promised to "obey" their husbands and each tried to explain that there was still something collaborative about marriage and that they made most decisions together. Whatever they believed about their autonomy or their work, our mothers' authority as presider or copresider at the family dinner table was equally evident. Eventually my wife and I visited and ate at those two tables, and later each became family in the other's house. Though we noted the differences, both felt natural, and in each we felt our mother's legitimate personal force defining a life and its relationships. Both families' practice—whether it was father or mother who occupied the head of the table—modeled easy, intentional community-making that shaped family.

Two ritual leaders (both parents) were warmly present in making those distinct supper traditions. My wife and I both remember times of conflict and times of comfort at the table. We both acknowledge that family dinner formed us, and from those two tables, as we made two careers and leaned into all the challenges of our work and children's school schedules, we made and protected our own meal rituals for us and our children. Sitting down together, candles, prayer, lingering to talk. Those rituals continue with just the two of us.

Meal practice showed us parents enjoying their roles and each other. Both tables enacted shared parental leadership and authority. And at both tables, we felt and enjoyed a gracious authority that invited everyone at the table to talk and enjoy the meal together. Dependable ritual structures let the leaders of these family meal liturgies simply be themselves. Each way of gathering at the table made sense.

Writing today about women preaching and presiding at the liturgy, I remember these two household models and see no one concerned about who "ought to" preside or sit at the head of the table.

Both of our mothers were highly intelligent women. My mother-in-law had found her role as the wife of a diplomat turned international banker. She entertained when his work brought people home and held the household in order when he was away. My mother, with a Phi Beta Kappa in economics, was bookkeeper to my dad's medical practice.

As East Coast Episcopalians, my wife's parents, if they were alive today, would be surprised to see their family meal introduced as a way to consider any aspect of Holy Communion. In the 1950s for many Episcopalians, church and sacrament belonged to a different domain from household life. Each domain had its wholly distinct rules. And while Christian denominations in the 1950s were quite conscious of their differences, particularly ritual differences, all four parents at those tables would reflexively picture a *man* as "pastor" or "minister." In the same time, my wife's father, Yale 1939, was fiercely opposed to Yale going coed. That piece changed for him personally in 1970 when he realized his youngest daughter might carry on the family's Yale legacy.

It would seem odd to my father-in-law and mother-in-law to look back on family meal traditions seeking ritual or sacramental clues. But in the natural human order by which we gather to share a meal in our society, the blend of the two familys' sense of hospitality and feast helps me look and plan for good flow at the Eucharistic Table. I don't think it would have occurred to most Episcopal clergy in the 1950s to ask what family meals revealed for the more evidently "sacred" and apparently less personal unfolding of a service of Holy Communion.

Experiencing women presiding at our defining rituals was not the only thing that moved us to look for and foster pattern analogies between ritual and everyday life, but women in ministry has been one significant reason that we've begun to seek, acknowledge, and welcome the *personal* presence of presider, deacon, and congregational participants. Thinking over the forty years and women colleagues whose presiding has moved and touched me (or puzzled and disturbed me), I'm remembering particular people, not their liturgical quirks or special devotional practices, but the personal character of their presence at the Table, to the prayers, and to the whole community.

2.

In my seminary in the late 60s some faculty members still cultivated an impersonal, deliberately detached presence as presiders at the liturgy. It had been the norm on the Nashotah House and General Seminary end of liturgical spectrum. At General a hinted affectation of an English accent also helped. Virginia Seminary graduates I remember echoed Southern aristocratic accents, and their exaggerated enunciation and slightly sing-song "sincere" or "feeling" speaking of the prayers felt impersonal in a different way, but ultimately just as detached and formulaic. Whatever teaching may have accompanied that style, it also made the congregation witnesses while someone said prayers on their behalf.

In "Mass Class" we learned that the classic Anglican way asked a presider to make himself as transparent as glass so the sacrament itself could shine through. "No jewelry but a wedding ring," we were told. For this ideal, wristwatches were a dilemma. Perhaps a quiet, smaller watch with a dark leather band was all right, but nothing that attracted attention. But that was only half the story.

Something else emerged with the decade of Vatican II. In those early stages of our own liturgical reform, some of our teachers explicitly offered the possibility of a different kind of embodiment. I don't remember anyone framing the question quite this way, but in the post–Vatican II ecumenical church, we were beginning to wonder how a presider's specific human and personal presence was inevitably part of our sacramental experience.

In my seminary years, it's possible that everyone in my seminary class owned a dog-eared paperback copy of Edward Steichen's *The Family of Man*. Steichen's photo collection intended to offer the broadest diversity of men's and women's faces to proclaim the universality of human experience. Our specific humanity wasn't the problem, but a gift. And the specific humanity of the other was gift too. Despite its title, *The Family of Man* brought fresh, optimistic perspective to humanity and an eloquent wordless plea for ending divisions. Photos showed universal humanity that was specific and diverse. The humanity of the incarnation took on different faces with different people and moments.

Michael Polanyi's *Personal Knowledge: Towards a Post-Critical Philosophy* (1958) was new and on our minds. Mass class itself pointed us to wondering how it might or would be to hear a woman's voice singing the Eucharistic prayer or preaching her experience from the pulpit. While we, an entirely male seminary class, began talking (because of our own diversity, and because the Stonewall Inn on Christopher Street was just over a mile away) about whether or how a presider might come out as homosexual or for that matter, a heterosexual young man, our sisters, girlfriends, or wives making their own sense of the women's movement threatened what we thought we knew of church.

3.

In the mid–1980s, after I'd been ordained a dozen years, the Presbytery of San Jose authorized me, an Episcopal priest, to join the teaching elders of that presbytery ordaining my mother a Presbyterian minister. After her ordination I had the startling privilege of being a senior colleague to my mother who for her first couple of years regularly called me to think through new pastoral challenges and liturgical questions. In those same years, my dad described how much he was learning from being in gatherings where he was "Nancy's husband" after mother's forty years of being "Harold's wife," or "Dr. Schell's wife."

Two decades later, I was a guest at the Saturday gathering of the same presbytery, when my mother completed her term as moderator. That Saturday she presided at Eucharist, startling and moving me with how familiar it all felt. Vested in Presbyterian elder's black gown with a presider's stole over it, Mother prayed a full Eucharistic Prayer (not just the words of institution). The paten held a beautiful round loaf of leavened bread (not tiny cubes of Wonder Bread), and the chalice of wine replaced little cups of grape juice.

The opening phrase in our 1979 Book of Common Prayer, "The Holy Eucharist, the principal act of Christian worship on the Lord's Day . . ." was borrowed verbatim from the Presbyterian *Book of Order.* When the Presbyterians wrote those words, like the Episcopal liturgists drafting our prayer book, they were promoting an as yet unrealized ideal. Through the same forty years that we've been ordaining women priests in our church (like the Presbyterians, UCC, Lutherans, and more), our church has become more attentive to ritual and more Eucharistically centered.

When those who opposed the ordination of women questioned how a woman could represent Christ as priest at the altar, they were appealing to a deeply embedded principle of scholastic sacramental theology. What's needed to confect a valid celebration of the Eucharist: bread, wine, a validly ordained priest saying "the words of institution," oh, yes, and a congregation.

We may still be accustomed to look for glimpses of a Last Supper reenactment in what the priest does at the altar. Oddly, the Protestant Reformation left that bit of scholasticism intact. In that way of thinking, developed in medieval scholasticism, the "words of institution" stand out as the sacramental heart of the Eucharistic Prayer. For both Reformation and Counter-Reformation theologians, the presider's role at Holy Communion was to read Jesus's words of institution over bread and wine. On the Reformation side, no one seemed to notice that the agreement that the presider was *Alter Christus,* "Another Christ," persisted. HIS job was to stand at the table for US and say, "This is MY body. . . . This is MY blood."

As two generations have shifted our expectations to much more frequent Communion, ecumenical Protestant and some post–Vatican II Roman Catholic thinking have steadily converged in a renewed Eucharistic practice that moves our attention from the presider as "Another Christ" to the whole gathered assembly being and becoming the body of Christ together.

The gathered people together are (and by the Spirit becoming) the body of Christ. Leading us in becoming who we are, the presider in her (or his) particular humanity embodies US, one specific presence in our many distinctive, diverse presences to one another. S/he prays in our voice (whether s/he is soprano, baritone, or somewhere in between) as we share in our gathered prayer and action. This shift in emphasis back toward ancient roots usefully challenges our thinking about Christian formation in the liturgy, though some bemoan a loss of Eucharistic devotion.

4.

Just two years before the Philadelphia ordinations, Virginia Satir's book *Peoplemaking* brought family systems thinking to a wide audience. Satir was telling America that becoming fully human happened inevitably within a human system, that human personhood and wholeness were a community work in progress. "The family," she said, "is a microcosm, by knowing how to heal the family, I know how to heal the world." With Rabbi Edwin Friedman's *Generation to Generation* (1985), many Episcopal Church leaders began to observe how healing congregational systems could open us to Spirit for healing the world.

The presider's particular humanity, who that person is to us, how we glimpse them in a human context, matters to us as we've begun to know ourselves as persons in contexts, human in our family and organizational systems. Over these forty years I've known something new of Spirit in myself from the particular praying I've heard in this or that woman's or man's voice speaking or singing the prayer regularly, in her face praying a part of the Eucharistic prayer that's particularly alive for us, or in her voice and touch receiving Communion from her.

These changes all contribute to a different experience of Eucharist, of the community, and of Jesus's presence with us, and that different experience contributes to and belongs to a startling, broad shift among liberal Protestants and Roman Catholics in our practice and rule of common prayer.

A presbyteral collegium that includes both men and women begins to free us from an old normal of neutered or feminized ("darling, your dress is divine, but your purse is on fire") male clergy. Seemingly trivial clues can point to larger discoveries and truths. For example, over the past forty years of seeing women preaching and presiding, it seems we've heard less and less discussion of what the vestments don't cover—the height of heels on a woman's shoes or visible earrings or other jewelry. In the same forty years, haven't we seen more bearded male clergy at the table and more running shoes cowboy boots under an alb?

5.

Meanwhile, with all this change we've come to a broad scholarly consensus that the words of Institution were simply absent from the second-century Didache Eucharistic Prayer (the earliest we have) and from the third-century prayer of Saints Addai and Mari. I was startled and quite intrigued in a conversation with the Benedictine liturgical scholar Godfrey Diekmann to hear his theory that the words of institution had made their way into liturgical use first as words of administration. When I passed that word on to St. Lydia's Dinner Church, a new Lutheran and Episcopal congregation in Brooklyn, they began experimenting with saying Jesus's words to one another as they share Eucharist, "This is my body," "This is my blood," or "This is my body given for you." What a holy, disarming experience to have someone say those words to you as they offer you bread and wine, and then to turn to the next person and say the words oneself! For a very long time we've described ourselves as "an Incarnational church," but saying Jesus's words to another person takes incarnation to a startlingly new dimension of personal embodiment—my body and yours, your body and mine.

In the same forty years that many Protestant churches have become more liturgical and more Eucharistically centered, some conservative Roman Catholics would tell you the Roman church has become "less Catholic." Both observations point to a church that is both startlingly local and universal in a new way. Women presiding at the table and administering Communion figures as one part of an enormous shift in how WE together and individually are present to Christ and in Christ with and in the assembled Eucharistic community.

The old *Alter Christus* understanding is still pervasive in so many ways and so shapes our unconscious expectations that we may sometimes miss seeing what's replacing it.

As accustomed as we are to hearing the presider shift to the first person as s/he quotes Jesus's words, do we notice that when s/he prays, "This is my body. . . . This is my blood," that it sounds like s/he is speaking of his/her own very self and the body before us? Our eyes and ears don't hear quotation marks. S/he speaks as Jesus offering us his Body and Blood in bread and wine.

We diverge from our Roman Catholic sisters and brothers who have explicitly added "male" to their canonical descriptions of the priest, but the Chicago-Lambeth Quadrilateral (1888) holds up as essential the old but not original practice of someone speaking the words of institution in the Eucharistic prayer, "the Supper of the Lord—ministered with unfailing use of Christ's words of institution and of the elements ordained by Him." It's time to question that "unfailing use." Does this ancient but not original norm direct our vision away from the living, breathing body of Christ assembled? How do we give thanks on behalf of all and for all and discover ourselves becoming Christ's body differently if our prayers, like the Didache and Addai and Mari, don't have a presider speaking as Christ and reenacting the Last Supper?

6.

I haven't been able to find the exact date we first thrilled to Corita Kent's brightly colored print proclaiming, "A Man Fully Alive Is the Glory of God," though by its noninclusive language, we can guess that her serigraph of these words from Irenaeus of Lyons dates from about the same time as our Episcopal Church's first ordinations of women as priests when our ear for gendered language and disquiet at generic use of "man" in the liturgy was still gaining momentum. Almost as quickly as Corita's serigraph brought Irenaeus's statement to people's attention, people began correcting the male language, quoting Irenaeus in the more familiar, further paraphrase, "The glory of God is *a human being fully alive.*"

We can be grateful to Corita for making Irenaeus's words known to so many people, and for the crowd-sourced correction that kept the text before us. "Human being" is unquestionably what Irenaeus meant. "Fully alive" may be both more and less than he meant, though the post-Corita paraphrase, "a human being fully alive," certainly offers a useful theme statement for our forty years' experience of women in ordained presbyteral ministry. Irenaeus's original, more naked declaration, that "the glory of God is a living man [human] and the life of man [humans] is the vision of God," implies that God's glory is in each and every human life and that all human life is the vision of God. That incipient universalism speaks with a new urgency in the twenty-first century in part thanks to the experience we've had of learning to preside at the Altar Table as specific men and women.

Specific men and women represent and speak for us in the pulpit or at the Altar Table. For any of us, our living humanity, the glory of God has as many different voices and different kinds of voices as we've experienced in different presiders.

Sr. Corita's paraphrase emphasized our call to full humanity in Irenaeus's words, the call her art consistently celebrated with her palette of bold colors and by the texts she chose and paraphrased or wrote. Like Virginia Satir, she implied a process of discovery and growth inherent in becoming fully human. Is it a coincidence that the first two witnesses I thought of for this lifelong process of change and formation were women? Yes, a moment's thought can readily name men like Carl Jung, Jean Piaget, or Erik Erikson. So women and men teachers both have challenged and inspired us to see human developmental stages through the span of our lives. But remembering the strident and sometimes terrified voices of opponents to the ordination of women, I wonder whether they had an intuitive grasp of how inescapably evident the stages and moments of human growth would be when a woman stood at the Altar Table.

Certainly development epiphanies appear in what we've said and heard over forty years of seeing women presiding at the Altar Table. Here's a tiny sampling of a recognizable cluster of experiences, moments of discovery and healing (or upset and confusion) we've felt or heard responding to seeing a specific human someone (and now, we can say, a woman or a man) gathering us, interpreting Scripture, and speaking our experience of Good News in preaching and leading prayer at the Table:

> "I cried the first time I received Communion from a woman."
>
> "Our priest was visibly pregnant in her vestments on Christmas Eve, and I thought . . ."
>
> "Did you notice he was wearing tennis shoes?"
>
> "She's holding her baby on her hip when she's at the altar!"
>
> "His toddler climbs the steps and stands alongside him at the altar."
>
> "I just kept watching her long, dangly earrings, and it didn't feel like praying."
>
> "S/He's in a wheelchair and all we can see when s/he's behind the altar is his/her head."

7.

A Jesuit friend exactly my age remembered planning a mass with a university ritual studies class. It was about the time of the Philadelphia ordinations. A Roman Catholic objected angrily to his undeclared assumption that the presider had to be a male. My friend decided to call her bluff and said, "All right, you're the presider." But as he made quick calculations about how one of the validly ordained Roman Catholic priests in the class could offer his canonical part in the consecration while allowing the woman to lead the assembly from the Altar Table, she'd already set to work sharing out leadership roles among everyone present, including him.

"I thought I was taking a bold risk as I scrambled to find some way to respond to her protest of hierarchical ordering of church, but she showed me how far short my understanding of a role I thought I owned and could delegate and manage stopped before really revisioning the church and community. She wasn't demanding that women have a place in an old hierarchy, she was aching for shared leadership and collaboration."

When our church began ordaining women to the priesthood, were we embracing shared and collaborative leadership? Does my friend's appreciative and contrite reflection on this decades' old experience tell us something about women in liturgical leadership? Or is it that he and she were caught in the same current of change, the same identical stirring of the Spirit?

Becoming persons is the work of the Spirit among us. The work goes on. Our diocesan convention asked a fourteen-year-old youth delegate to tell the convention what she thought would keep young people active in Episcopal churches. She was ready for this question, speaking from her experience of a liturgy that's begun to shape itself in embrace of the person—"Welcome us to church as real participants and give us real work to do—sure, we can light candles, but how about letting us help administer Communion or read the Gospel?"

DONALD SCHELL has served as a college chaplain (Episcopal Church at Yale), a small town vicar (St. David's, Caldwell, Idaho), and, with Rick Fabian, founded St. Gregory of Nyssa Episcopal Church, San Francisco. His embodied, personal practice includes daily Aikido (Second Degree

Black Belt), frequent Music that Makes Community workshops (a movement he founded with musician friends to recover preliterate practices of teaching and leading music). Donald was a founding member of the Coordinating Council of Spiritual Directors International and a council member and sometime president of Associated Parishes for Liturgy and Mission. With his daughter Maria, he wrote *My Father, My Daughter: Pilgrims on the Road to Santiago* (Church Publishing) after they walked the pilgrimage across Spain to Santiago de Compostela. His new book *Word Made Flesh* (LeaderResources) is a hands-on, practical manual teaching people how to design and lead improvised scriptural dramas with congregants in the liturgy.

CHAPTER 4

"Mid-Wives to Justice": Redefining Pastoral Theology

Sheryl A. Kujawa-Holbrook

Sociologists and theological educators suggest that women's entry into the ordained ministry represents the most significant transformation in pastoral leadership in the twentieth century, if not since the Reformation.[1] Without a doubt the events of July 1974 transformed my own life. Forty years is not a long time in historical terms to assess the impact of the ordination of women on the patterns of religious leadership within The Episcopal Church. At the time, many hoped that the church, too, would be transformed. One of the Philadelphia 11, Carter Heyward writes in her book *A Priest Forever* (1976): "*I see women as the single most creative force for renewal within the Christian Church. We, as a group, are those challenged most immediately with the task of renewal*—of making new what is old—within and beyond ourselves in the Church and elsewhere."[2]

Have we lived into the promise of those days, and if not, where do we fall short of that dream? How has women's ordination influenced the shape of religious leadership within the church, as well as ministerial practice? How has women's ordination affected pastoral care? Suzanne Radley Hiatt, also ordained with the Philadelphia 11,

---

1 Joy McDougall, "Weaving Garments of Grace: En-gendering a Theology of Call to Ordained Ministry for Women Today," *Theological Education* 39, no. 2 (2003): 150.
2 Carter Heyward, *A Priest Forever* (Cleveland: Pilgrim Press, 2000), 3.

and a pastoral theologian, noted in 1985, the year of my own ordination: "If women enter the public world in great numbers but don't change the way things are done, then there really is no gain for anyone. Indeed, there is a net loss, for the women who used to carry the burden of volunteer community service are no longer available to do that. Being 'the best man' is a losing proposition for both women and society."[3]

Pastoral theology, also known as practical theology, is one field where the impact of women's experience (and that of other marginalized persons) within ministry and society is a major source of theological reflection and ministerial practice. *"We are called to tell our stories,* and in telling our stories *we manifest a new reality,"* writes Heyward. "We pick up where our sisters Mary Magdalene, Joanna, Mary the mother of James, and the other women who witnessed the Resurrection left off. With them, we tell of our theological experience, our relationship to God."[4] The field gained prominence in the 1960s and 1970s—the same era as the ordination of women to the diaconate and priesthood in The Episcopal Church—through the increased interest in the relationship between psychology and religion. Women scholars and practitioners have played key roles in the development of pastoral theology as a field. As a field of scholarship, it has historically been on the margins of the academy.

More recently, pastoral theology has become more interdisciplinary and the emphasis has shifted from individual pastoral care to community-based care defined within the wider religious, social, and political context. Pastoral theologian Bonnie J. Miller-McLemore argues that the movement of the field from an individual to a "communal contextual" paradigm is largely due to the growing presence of women in the field.[5] Pastoral theologians such as Miller-McLemore and Christine Cozad Neuger redefined the field by writing widely about the communal nature of pastoral care, and the role of the pastor *"as one who conspires and collaborates with others in the struggle to bring forth new life from the creative tensions 'on the boundary.'"*[6]

---

3 Quoted from Suzanne Radley Hiatt papers, Union Theological Seminary, 1985.
4 Heyward, *Priest Forever,* 3. Emphasis added.
5 Bonnie J. Miller-McLemore, "The Human Web: Reflections on the State of Pastoral Theology," in *Through the Eyes of Women: Insights For Pastoral Care,* ed. Jeanne Stevenson Moessner (Philadelphia: Westminster John Knox, 1996), 9–26.
6 Christie Cozad Neuger, *The Arts of Ministry: Feminist-Womanist Approaches* (Louisville: Westminster John Knox, 1996), 11. Emphasis added.

In the Anglican-Episcopal tradition, pastoral theology is rooted in the image of the Incarnation. The primary task of pastoral theology, that is ministry, is not limited to techniques or skills. Rather, it is about *the kind* of people we are, and it is deeply theological. *All* are made in the image of God; God is present within us, and we are present to God. Pastoral theologians within the Anglican-Episcopal tradition frame community life through Scripture, reason, tradition (and experience) in a spirit of prayer. All are tools for discernment. Within the Anglican-Episcopal tradition, the created order is good; God assumed a human body, and is active throughout the course of human history. Our pastoral theology and the practice of pastoral care is embodied in our worship, and framed by the Book of Common Prayer, from birth to death. As Christians in the Anglican-Episcopal tradition, we participate in transformative rituals which express our deepest concerns, memories, and longings. Through our prayers within the body of the church, we all share in the Incarnation, and we are all empowered through baptism to participate in healing, empowering, liberating ministry. Anglican-Episcopal pastoral theology bespeaks the global interdependence of humankind and all creation. It is not enough to work for the healing of individuals; we are also called to work for reconciliation within our communities and throughout the world.

Pastoral theology is intimately concerned with care of the marginalized and oppressed within our midst; it is about lived theology, congregational life, ministerial practice, and social justice. Theologically, the focus of pastoral theology is on the "beloved community" or the love of God actualized in the midst of life's struggles and transformational practice. Pastoral theologian Carol Lakey Hess describes feminist approaches to pastoral theology, rooted in both the academy and faith communities, as "becoming mid-wives to justice."[7] Jeanne Stevenson Moessner utilizes the image a "living human *web*" as a guiding metaphor for pastoral theology.[8] Because of this focus on relationships-in-community, pastoral theology addresses racism, sexism, heterosexism, ableism, ageism, classism, religious oppression, and colo-

---

7 Carol Lakey Hess, "Becoming Mid-Wives to Justice: A Feminist Approach to Practical Theology," in *Liberating Faith Practices: Feminist Practical Theologies in Context,* ed. Denise Ackerman and Riet Bons-Storm (Leuven: Peeters, 1998), 51.
8 Jeanne Stevenson Moessner, *Through the Eyes of Women: Insights for Pastoral Care* (Minneapolis: Fortress Press, 1996), 16.

nialism, as well as other issues that impact both the church and the wider society. Moreover, women pastoral theologians, whether focused on spiritual care, religious education, worship, preaching, or other subfields, raise the awareness that every pastoral action is a political action, either complicit with, or in opposition to, systemic oppression.[9]

Within theological education, pastoral theology often serves as the bridge between theology and practice and faith communities and the academy. We live in a world today characterized by deep spiritual hunger. The capacity to form communities, to build bridges across difference, is a crucial skill in a world where all people need each other to survive. In many ways, the field of pastoral theology is also a bridge between feminist and womanist theory and theology. The feminist and womanist values of human interconnectedness and interdependence are crucial if we are going to build bridges between human need and communities of care.

The 1990s brought a significant increase not only in the numbers of women practical theologians, but also in writings that challenged gender oppression in theology and ministry.[10] Pastoral theologians writing out of the "second wave" of feminism in the latter part of the twentieth century highlighted the importance of women's experience and the enduring realities of exclusion in church and society. Some brought together theological reflection with women's experiences, such as child-bearing, eating disorders, and breast cancer, in an effort to raise consciousness about the centrality of these experiences. Others discussed the importance of examining God images and gender exclusive liturgical language as a means of challenging patriarchy within religious structures. For more than a generation, such pastoral theologians have joined voices with other scholars and practitioners to address the problems of violence against women and children in religious institutions and the family, and have pushed for increased accountability and prevention, as well as to a revised theological understanding about the sources of violence rooted in patriarchy and gendered hierarchy.[11]

---

9 Christine Cozad Neuger, "Pastoral Counseling as an Art of Personal Political Activism," in *The Arts of Ministry: Feminist-Womanist Approaches* (Louisville: Westminster John Knox, 1996), 88–117.

10 Jeanne Hoeft, "Gender, Sexism, and Heterosexism," in *The Wiley-Blackwell Companion to Practical Theology*, ed. Bonnie J. Miller-McLemore (Malden, MA: Wiley-Blackwell, 2012), 412.

11 Hoeft, "Gender, Sexism and Heterosexism," 413–15.

Throughout the history of the United States, women and men of color justly criticized white middle-class feminism as racist, exclusive, and irrelevant. However, the legacy of pastoral theologians suggests a broader and more profound use of the term "feminist." Within pastoral theology, feminism is not limited to equality between men and women, or the achievement of equal rights for white middle-class women, though both are important. Rather, within the field of pastoral theology, feminism is built on a critical analysis of unjust structures and based on analysis of the interlocking nature of oppression. In this regard, feminism recognizes not only the need to eliminate sexism, but also challenges racist, classist, and hetero-sexist biases, along with all other forms of oppression. An understanding of interlocking oppressions completely transforms pastoral theology and pastoral practice. It raises questions about who we care for, how we care for them, and how our own social location impacts ministerial practice. It not only emphasizes the importance of social location and context, but it advocates for pastoral practice rooted in collaboration and partnership. As Jeanne Stevenson Moessner notes, "To think about pastoral theology and care from [a feminist] vantage point requires prophetic, transformative challenges to systems of power, authority, and domination that continue to violate, terrorize, and systematically destroy individuals and communities."[12]

Over the past thirty years pastoral theologians, influenced by feminist, womanist, and liberation theologies, have challenged privatized approaches to pastoral care, counseling, and ministry, arguing that these approaches privilege the middle-class, white, male, Western origins of the pastoral care and counseling movement. In other words, is it the role of pastoral theology to help people adjust to their circumstances, or is the goal to empower them to fight injustice? Such perspectives challenge those in ministry to understand the social context of suffering and hope. Donald M. Chinula, in his 1997 work on the foundations for pastoral care found in the works of Dr. Martin Luther King Jr., writes that "hyper-individualistic" models of pastoral care are not only irrelevant to most of the world's people, but they are dangerous in that they obscure the sociocultural sources of poverty and the related racism, sexism, classism, etc. "It imposes guilt and shame on the help seeker," he writes. "It leaves untreated the toxic

---

12 Moessner, *Through the Eyes of Women,* 16.

and stressing socio-cultural forces from whence distressed persons come and to which treated individuals return. It makes it difficult for those most needing help to afford existing services. . . . Because of its primary focus on the individual, the hyper-individualistic model lacks serious critical social theory and analysis to inform its praxis."[13]

Several pastoral theologians writing after 2000 have broadened the concept of pastoral care in ways which examine the impact of marginalization and oppression on various groups. The work of British pastoral theologian Emmanuel Y. Lartey places pastoral care within a global context and stresses the importance of social location in the midst of the life experiences of the suffering, the poor, and the oppressed.[14] Sheryl Kujawa-Holbrook and Karen B. Montago assume that the bias of most faith traditions is with the marginalized: "God sees, hears, knows and lives in the midst of the poor and the oppressed. The primary work of faith communities, then, is human *freedom*—to provide an opportunity for freedom for all people."[15] Other pastoral theologians such as Tapiwa N. Mucherera examine the impact of colonialism on indigenous communities in Africa and elsewhere throughout the world, wherein the culture, values, religion, and humanity of peoples is marginalized. Using narrative methodologies, Mucherera writes: "Revillaging, religion, and reauthoring are the main signposts for the future in these contexts faced with horrendous suffering from poverty and HIV/AIDS."[16]

Concerns about gender oppression in theology and religious institutions continue as a global issue. Gender oppression impacts the most intimate aspects of human life: open expression, physical safety, clothing, relationship, and control over movement. Contributions to the field from queer theory and practice have expanded the categories of gender and sexuality. Where we once assumed that sexuality was biological, and gender was the social construction of norms, the binary categories of female and male once assumed are now

---

13 Donald M. Chinula, *Building King's Beloved Community: Foundations for Pastoral Care and Counseling with the Oppressed* (Cleveland: United Church Press, 1997), xvii–xix.

14 Emmanuel Y. Lartey, *In Living Color: An Intercultural Approach to Pastoral Care and Counseling* (London: Jessica Kingsley, 2003), 124–25.

15 Sheryl A. Kujawa-Holbrook and Karen B. Montagno, *Taking Oppression Seriously in Pastoral Care* (Minneapolis: Fortress, 2009), 2.

16 Tapiwa N. Mucherera, *Meet Me at the Palaver: Narrative Pastoral Counseling in Postcolonial Contexts* (Eugene, OR: Cascade Books, 2009), x.

questioned. British practical theologian Elaine Graham moves beyond arguments citing gender as either biological fact or social construction, suggesting instead that it is a "cultural artifact." In so doing, Graham shifts the discussion to ethical principles by which church and society support particular gender patterns and marginalize others.[17]

Interestingly, while men are also gendered, and negatively affected by sexism, there are comparatively few texts such as *The Care of Men* (1997) by Christie Neuger and James Poling that address the impact of sexism (and heterosexism) on them. Although the numbers of works in pastoral theology directly focused on men's experience are increasing, many continue to assume that gender is a category that only affects women. At the same time, growth since the mid-1990s in the field of "body theology," predominately under the leadership of women and gay men, argues the need to transcend Christian theologies that negate or deny the body as a sacred space, rather than as an expression of the incarnate God in the world. Body theology both embraces the social order and considers the body and its experiences to be a site of divine revelation. "One of the aims of body theology is to help the church to construct a new anthology, a new understanding of human nature, that recognizes the centrality of embodiment," write British theologians Lisa Isherwood and Elizabeth Stuart. "Profanity is not the failure to open oneself up to outside intervention but rather the failure to love passionately all that we see, touch, taste, smell and hear."[18]

As this brief survey suggests, pastoral theologians from the 1970s to the present not only addressed issues pertaining to gender and other forms of marginalization, but in doing so, contributed to movements that changed the definition and focus of pastoral leadership today. Some of the ongoing themes include:

1. The need to take seriously the interlocking nature of oppression.

Most women continue to encounter injustice due to sexism, and yet the impact of oppression was (and is now) not borne by all women *equally*. While gender is *always* an issue, it is not always *the* issue in

---

17 Elaine Graham, *Gender, Personhood, and Theology* (Minneapolis: Fortress Press, 1996).
18 Lisa Isherwood and Elizabeth Stuart, *Introducing Body Theology* (Cleveland: Pilgrim Press, 1998), 148–49.

every given context. No form of oppression stands alone, but is linked to the many forms of identity we incarnate as our social location—race, ethnicity, social class, language, sexual identity, immigration status, physical ability. All impact accessibility to exercise pastoral leadership in the church and in the world. Marginalization continues within groups of women, including women of color, poor women, working class women, lesbian women, transgender women, old women, young women, and others.

2. The importance of embodiment within theologies and pastoral practice.

In keeping with the doctrine of the Incarnation, which asserts that God became flesh, pastoral theology seeks to offer body-affirming care for women and LGBTQI persons who experience body-related oppression in church and society. Although the body has been considered something to overcome for generations of Christians, body-centered pastoral theologies stress the importance of breaking through traditional body-spirit dualisms, instead recognizing the sacredness of the body and the whole created order.

3. Authentic pastoral leadership is always rooted in community.

Today pastoral theologians stress that all ministry is inherently collaborative, not competitive. Every member is endowed with gifts for ministry in creation and through the Spirit. Identifying and celebrating one another's gifts builds up the body. Such ministry values accountability, rather than control, and interdependence, rather than delegation. It seeks the enhancement of the individual and the community, and values learning over productivity or success. Authentic pastoral leadership facilitates and encourages mutual flourishing, beyond the rigid confines of traditional institutional roles and boundaries.

4. The authority for all ministries comes with baptism.

The impact of clericalism on women's ministries, and ministry in general, remains a live issue. Has women's ordination brought with it a transformed vision of ministry, or does it reinscribe models of ministry rooted in a "clergy-centric" church culture? All ministries are baptismal, and all members of the church are called to ministry in their daily lives and work, not just inside church walls. Ordained persons are called to sign and order particular aspects of the ministry in which all the members have a share. Today, the five questions of the baptismal covenant in the prayer book provide a framework for looking at the priesthood of all believers as key to baptismal identity. The fact that in many cases in The Episcopal Church, women's ordination has served to limit, not enhance, vocational choices for lay-women is an indication not only of clericalism, but of a theology of ministry based in religious hierarchy rather than in the priesthood of all believers. Authority for ministry for all women and men comes first from our baptism, not from ordination. All baptized persons are called to share in the work of Christ as prophet, priest, and leader.

5. *The foundations of prayer and spiritual practice.*

The need for a disciplined life of prayer is fundamental to pastoral leadership. Transformative ritual practice facilitates the pastoral vision of the church in the world. There are many different styles and disciplines for personal prayer, and growth as a ministering community is enhanced by exploring and respecting the varieties of personal spirituality. There is also a need for congregations and other groups to develop patterns of prayer and spiritual rules of life that include more than Sunday liturgical worship. Spiritual practices such as inclusive language and same-sex blessings, to name a few, are so powerful because they connect spiritual yearning with pastoral care through transformative ritual.

6. *Act locally, think globally.*

The global reality of The Episcopal Church today is deeply indebted to women's ministries. Historically, women's pastoral leadership exercised within the home was expanded in the nineteenth century to include reform movements, religious education, missionary activities, and leadership in religious organizations. There would be little or no mission work in The Episcopal Church without women's expansive vision, commitment, organizational expertise, and willingness to give their money to these ministries. Similarly, many medical, social welfare, and educational institutions were founded and staffed by volunteer and professional women. It was primarily women who developed the fields of religious education, higher education chaplaincy, and health care chaplaincy within the Episcopal congregations and missions located throughout the world. Pastoral theology is no longer confined to those within our own churches, but is part of a global vision concerned with the care for our sisters and brothers who live in other parts of the world, as well as all creatures that inhabit the earth.

One of the great legacies of the Philadelphia 11, and of Episcopal women throughout history, is their ability to be persistent; to hold the church accountable to the people that constitute it. For all the attempts to diminish or dismiss their ministries, women still manage to profoundly impact those around them precisely because their lives had so much meaning. That women accomplished so much and created so many meaningful roles for themselves with limited support is testament to the depth of their faith and indomitable spirits.

As the people of God, we are called during these troubling times to respond to a world groaning under the weight of broken relationships. We are called at this time to use all the gifts we have available to transform our church and be about the healing and wholeness the whole world craves. In this fateful time, how will we prepare the next generations of ministers of the gospel? What responsibility have we assumed for confronting the lessons of the past? In what condition shall the next generation find our heritage? And what shall we hand over to them? Will they perceive the love of Christ in our work and in our lives? Will they see hope and joy in the midst of struggle? The empowerment *of all* in The Episcopal Church today is dependent on our capacity to redefine pastoral leadership. Change will come only through the enactment of new models of the church as the whole people of God; models grounded in shared ministry and mutual respect.

SHERYL A. KUJAWA-HOLBROOK is a priest of the Episcopal Diocese of Los Angeles, an educator, historian of religion, and practical theologian. She is currently vice president of academic affairs, dean of the faculty, and professor of practical theology at Claremont School of Theology and professor of Anglican studies at Bloy House, the Episcopal Theological School at Claremont. In addition to thirty years of experience as a teacher, trainer, spiritual director, chaplain, and workshop, conference, and retreat leader, she is the author of thirteen books and numerous articles and reviews. Her works related to Episcopal women's history, ministry, and pastoral theology include: *Deeper Joy: Laywomen and Vocation in the 20ᵗʰ Century Episcopal Church,* with Fredrica Harris Thompsett (2005); *Injustice and the Care of Souls: Pastoral Care with Marginalized Communities,* with Karen B. Montagno (2009); and *Born of Water, Born of Spirit: Supporting the Ministry of the Baptized in Small Congregations,* with Fredrica Harris Thompsett (2010).

CHAPTER 5

The Impact on the Church of England and Wider Anglican Communion

Jane Shaw

A Preacher Comes to Town

It was on April 9, 1978, that I first heard a female priest preach in a church in England. The church was St. Peter Mancroft in Norwich, a big church in the center of the city, and my parish. The priest was Canon Mary Michael Simpson, a canon at the Cathedral of St. John the Divine in New York City. The sermon had a big impact on me; or rather, I should say, the visual imagery of a female priest in the pulpit was what really had an effect. In fact, I have no memory of the sermon, and the rector commented in the parish bulletin, the *Mancroft Review*, the week after Canon Simpson had preached: "Those who judge sermons by length rather than quality will no doubt be in favour of the ordination of women. Canon Mary Simpson's sermon at Family Service on April 9th was timed at just over four minutes, certainly under five!"[1] The event was historic; the content of the sermon secondary.

I was just fifteen years old, active in the church, and, while most of my contemporaries were lining up for the autographs of teenage pop stars, it was Canon Simpson's autograph that I wanted that

---

1 *Mancroft Review* (monthly parish newsletter of St. Peter Mancroft, Norwich: May 1978).

Sunday. She was gracious, signed my order of service and offered an encouraging word. I still have that autographed bulletin somewhere in a box of teenage treasures.

What was the context into which Canon Simpson was preaching that Sunday in 1978?

The Church of England was proceeding slowly on the issue of ordained women, as it had done for many decades—producing reports and desultory debates about them. The first movements for the ordination of women had been formed in the interwar years, especially through the energy and commitment of activists like Maude Royden. The years after World War II had seen good work being done by deaconesses on the ground but, as Margaret Webster notes, "At 'the centre,' however, reports continued to be produced. The roll-call is depressing."[2] The uncertain status of deaconesses and their ministry remained.

Meanwhile, other parts of the Anglican Communion were moving more swiftly. Bishop James Pike, the radical bishop of California, ordained a woman, Phyllis Edwards, as a deacon rather than a deaconess in Grace Cathedral in 1968—without prior permission from the General Convention of The Episcopal Church. This action had pressed not only General Convention to discuss the matter, but also the bishops gathered at the Lambeth Conference that year to reach a decision recommending that all deaconesses be admitted to the diaconate. Lambeth resolutions are not binding, so it was up to individual provinces to consider whether they would follow that recommendation. The churches of Canada, Hong Kong, Kenya, Korea, and the United States quickly did so.

That same Lambeth Conference in 1968 declared the evidence for or against the ordination of women as priests to be inconclusive and sent the question out to the provinces for debate. The Anglican Consultative Council (known as the ACC, and at that time newly formed to consider controversial issues—like women's ordination—in the Communion) ratified this. Hong Kong led the way, which was not surprising, given that Florence Li Tim-Oi had been ordained there in 1944 in response to a pastoral need in the area where she was serving. She had, by the request of the Archbishop of Canterbury, stepped

---

2 Margaret Webster, *A New Strength, A New Song. The Journey to Women's Priesthood* (London: Mowbray, 1994), 25.

down from her position after World War II, but she did not resign her orders. In 1971 her priesthood was once again restored, and Jane Hwang and Joyce Bennett were ordained priest, with the approval (by twenty-four votes to twenty-two) of the ACC. While Hong Kong got on with things, the Church of England used the request for discussion in the provinces as an opportunity for another report; this time one produced by the energetic and formidable Christian Howard, who had learnt activism from her suffragist mother.

Meanwhile, in the United States, General Convention rejected motions for the ordination of women as priests in 1970 and again in 1973. Some women and bishops began to consider ordination without General Convention's permission and decided they would do it. In 1974, Robert DeWitt, the recently resigned bishop of Philadelphia, along with two other retired bishops, ordained eleven women as priests. Four more women were ordained as priests in Washington, DC, in 1975. Only in 1976 did General Convention vote to make women eligible for ordination to the priesthood and the episcopate. By this time, the Anglican Church in Canada had already voted to ordain women as priests (and indeed bishops) in 1975—a decision that was influential on General Convention's deliberations—and New Zealand followed in 1976.

Therefore, by the time Canon Simpson stepped into the pulpits of England in 1978, there were female priests in other parts of the Anglican Communion. The Church of England's General Synod had finally debated Christian Howards's report in July 1975, though "with all the enthusiasm of men and women asked to cross a mine-field wearing magnetic boots—and perhaps in the view of all sides—with the same results" as Sean Gill memorably expresses it.[3] Synod had passed a motion saying that there were no fundamental objections to the ordination of women to the priesthood; but a second motion, asking that legal barriers should be removed and legislation prepared, failed.

Despite this setback with the second motion, women and their supporters were keen, ready, and hopeful that Synod would decide to prepare and pass legislation soon. The institution, meanwhile, was fearful and cautious.

---

3 Sean Gill, *Women and the Church of England: From the Eighteenth Century to the Present* (London: SPCK, 1994), 251.

Priests from other parts of the Anglican Communion were beginning to visit the UK. One of the women irregularly ordained in Washington, DC, in 1975, Alison Palmer, had visited the University Church in Newcastle in 1977, at the invitation of the master of that church and chaplain to the university, Ian Harker, and had been invited to celebrate the Eucharist. This celebration was, by the church's canons, illegal. The bishop of the diocese, Ronald Bowlby, was a strong supporter of the ordination of women but was pressured to condemn the action. He did so, but in his statement he reminded people: "All of us need to remember that there is a long history of 'lawlessness' for conscience sake in the Church of England."[4]

So Canon Simpson was not the first American female priest to visit the Church of England. Nor was St. Peter Mancroft the only place where she preached on her 1978 trip. She also preached at York Minster, Manchester and Liverpool Cathedrals, Oxford and Cambridge university churches, and St. Martin in the Fields in London; and she was the first ordained woman to preach in Westminster Abbey. She and her sponsors—an informal network of men and women in the Church of England campaigning for the ordination of women, such as Margaret Webster, who was married to the dean of Norwich Cathedral and who probably made the connection to St. Peter Mancroft—were cautious in how they advertised her tour of England. It was probably also important, in terms of establishing a certain sense of legality that she was not one of the Philadelphia 11; and, to add to her respectable credentials, in the United States she was the first religious sister to be ordained a priest, and the first woman to be appointed a cathedral canon. The vicar of St. Peter Mancroft, David Sharp, in announcing in the *Mancroft Review* her upcoming visit, tried to take a carefully balanced position. "She [Canon Simpson] stresses that she is not here to engage in any controversy, nor particularly to promote women's ministry." But he continued to give what validation was possible: "Although she is not allowed to exercise her priestly ministry in the Church of England, she is welcome here as a preacher and accredited minister of the American Church, and we look forward to meeting her."[5] The balance expressed here speaks to the political shrewdness of David Sharp, who was a great supporter of women's

---

4 Webster, *New Strength*, 44.
5 *Mancroft Review* (Norwich: April 1978).

ordination, forward-thinking and innovative. In a private note to me much later, he admitted that he had not asked the (evangelical) bishop of Norwich's permission for Canon Simpson to preach. "I remember that I should have followed the rule in those days and asked Bishop Maurice Wood's permission to invite a preacher from outside, and especially such a controversial one, and I didn't, because I thought he would not approve. Of course, it hit the local paper, the *Eastern Daily Press*, and I heard he was not best pleased."[6]

The presence of female priests from overseas was significant that year, in the run up to a General Synod meeting when the issue was again on the agenda. In November 1978, Synod debated a motion that asked the standing committee to prepare and bring forward legislation for the ordination of women as priests and consecration as bishops. There was optimism it would pass. One hundred prominent laymen and women had published a declaration in favor of the ordination of women ahead of time, and the bishops were largely supportive. But the motion was defeated. As Margaret Webster put it: "Too many of the clergy were adamant, and too many of the laity were fearful."[7] It was in the silence following the announcement of this result that Deaconess Una Kroll famously shouted from the gallery: "We asked for bread and you gave us a stone."

The primary response to that vote was the creation of the Movement for the Ordination of Women in 1979, a national movement with its activism rooted in dioceses. I was sixteen years old and joined immediately.

The Long, Slow Road to Women's Ordination and Consecration in the Church of England

After that Synod defeat of 1978, it took another nine years for women to be ordained as deacons, and until 1992 for legislation to be passed for the ordination of women as priests. Women were finally ordained as priests in the Church of England in 1994, nineteen years after Synod had declared there were no fundamental objections to such a thing happening. General Synod has still not passed legislation for women to be ordained and consecrated to the episcopate, and—compared with

---

6 E-mail from Canon David Sharp to the author, November 24, 2013.
7 Webster, *New Strength*, 46.

the rest of the Anglican Communion—the Church of England now looks severely behind the times. After the consecration of Barbara Harris as suffragan bishop in Massachusetts in 1989, other provinces followed. In 1990, the first female diocesan was consecrated: Penny Jamieson in Dunedin, New Zealand. There are now female bishops in the United States, Canada, Cuba, Australia, New Zealand, Ireland, Southern Africa, and Southern India.

The Church of England's endless debates in Synod about the possibility of consecrating women as bishops looks out of tune not only with society but also, increasingly, the rest of the church. Certainly, such prevarication has contributed to the decline in credibility of the Church of England in the larger society, as indicated by November 2012 newspaper headlines from the day after General Synod's vote against legislation for female bishops by just six votes in the House of Laity. Rowan Williams, the outgoing archbishop of Canterbury, read the signs of the times, and told Synod after the vote that the Church of England had "a lot of explaining to do" to the church itself and to wider society. "We have as a result of yesterday undoubtedly lost a measure of credibility in our society," he said.[8] David Cameron, the prime minister, declared himself saddened by the vote and, answering a question at Prime Minister's Question Time in the House of Commons, said it was time for the Church of England "to get on with it" about female bishops.[9] Meanwhile, across the Pond, a headline in the *New York Times* read: "Veto on Female Bishops Leaves Anglicans in Crisis."[10] A week later, while preaching at his enthronement as bishop of Chichester, Martin Warner, one of the leading lights of the "traditionalist" camp opposed to the ordination of women, admitted that the rejection of female bishops had damaged the church.[11]

Why has it taken the Church of England so long? A comparison between the course taken by The Episcopal Church and that of the Church of England with respect to this issue may shed some light on this question.

---

8 http://www.theguardian.com/world/2012/nov/21/archbishop-church-vetoing-female-bishops.

9 http://www.theguardian.com/world/2012/nov/21/david-cameron-church-female-bishops.

10 http://www.nytimes.com/2012/11/22/world/europe/church-of-england-rejects-appointing-female-bishops.html?_r=0.

11 http://www.telegraph.co.uk/news/religion/9702076/Women-bishops-rejection-has-damaged-Church-traditionalist-bishop-admits.html.

In The Episcopal Church, men and women were willing to take the leap of conscience and this forced a response from the institution. The General Convention of The Episcopal Church had to respond to the "irregular" ordinations in Philadelphia and Washington, DC, at its meeting in 1976, just as it had been forced to consider the question of female deacons after Bishop Pike's actions at Grace Cathedral eight years earlier. In both cases, Convention's response was positive. When it came to debate the matter, it did so proactively: in 1968 it voted for female deacons; in 1976, it voted for women to be ordained to the priesthood and episcopate. There was opposition, but there was no capitulation, with the consequence that now, women have been ordained as priests in all 110 dioceses of The Episcopal Church; seventeen women have been elected and consecrated as bishops in the United States; and the presiding bishop is a woman—Katharine Jefferts Schori.

The Church of England has gone about things very differently. Those who worked for the ordination of women did so methodically, acting through the mechanisms and procedures of General Synod to achieve their result. This was a laborious process and was stretched out because the orders were split, in an unprecedented way: first deacons (1987), then priests (1992), and, whenever it comes, bishops. Synodical and parliamentary legislation had to be prepared and passed each time. (Because the Church of England is a state church, and the ordination of women is a change in the law of the land, legislation has to be passed by Parliament.) But this process was not just about slowness; it also broke the longstanding principle in Anglicanism that the three orders—deacon, priest, and bishop—should not be divided. As retired Bishop John Gladwin reminds us: "Women were ordained deacon and so brought into holy orders on the basis that they may not proceed to priesthood. Then when that barrier was removed in 1994, another was created to keep them from being called to the office of bishop in God's Church. There is no other incident in the history of the Church where such action has been pursued." He concludes: "The Church's present position on women bishops is illogical and untenable."[12] The irony is that while the Church hesitated about doing something new in ordaining women, it broke tradition by dividing the three-fold order of ministry in this way.

---

12 John Gladwin, "Women and the Integrity of Anglican Orders," in *The Call for Women Bishops* ed. Harriet Harris and Jane Shaw (London: SPCK, 2004), 67.

This division of the orders has been part of an attempt to hold things together, to go softly-softly, which at the same time has often meant not facing the question squarely, or deferring it. As Margaret Webster puts it, "Since 1984 the House of Bishops had supported the ordination of women as priests. Even in 1978, influenced by the Lambeth Conference, the majority had voted in favor. But they wanted that support to be consistent with a quiet life, and for many of them the policy had been to sidestep the questions at the heart of the matter."[13]

As a consequence, the Church of England, especially perhaps the bishops, capitulated to opposition. While all other churches in the Anglican Communion that have female priests (and in some cases female bishops) have dealt pastorally but informally with those opposed to the ordination of women, the Church of England decided it needed to cater to that opposition by creating "flying bishops" or Provisional Episcopal Visitors (PEV). This phenomenon came about *after* General Synod had voted for the ordination of women as priests in 1992, but before the legislation went to Parliament, and was an attempt by bishops to keep opponents in the church when some were vociferously threatening to leave (and when the Church of England had promised a 30,000 pounds payout to all who did leave). This synodical (not parliamentary) legislation enabled individual priests and parishes to choose the oversight of a PEV rather than their diocesan bishop. The Church of England has been much criticized for institutionalizing the opposition to female priests and setting a problematic precedent for the whole Anglican Communion by suggesting that oversight is no longer territorial but can, rather, be *issue* based. It paved the way for all kinds of groups to think that they can choose their own bishop; in the recent controversies about openly gay bishops, some churches have opted for oversight from bishops of other provinces, in a form of "border-crossing" that has been frowned upon but not disciplined.[14] There is an irony inherent in the Act of Synod: in order to maintain the tradition of a male-only priesthood in parts of the church for a small but vociferous minority, it broke with the longstanding tradition in the church that bishops should be appointed on the basis of territory rather than issue. The

---

13 Webster, *New Strength,* 192.
14 On PEVs and the Act of Synod, see the essays in Monica Furlong, ed., *Act of Synod, Act of Folly?* (London: SCM Press, 1998).

Act of Synod was intended to provide provincial Episcopal oversight; in reality it has provided *alternative* Episcopal oversight.

Furthermore, this set a precedent for how the Church of England went about considering the ordination and consecration of women as bishops. It started with the question "What do we do about the opponents?" rather than beginning with the more rational and obvious starting point, "How do we have women bishops?" Arguments about the exact nature of these provisions for opponents have for a long time held up this issue in Synod. Working groups have produced reports that have the mentality of "solving a problem" with a series of proposed compromises rather than proceeding with clarity and integrity, and in a straightforward way, to prepare legislation for women as bishops.[15] The all-male House of Bishops has presided over these working groups and reports with a sort of hand-wringing "Father knows best" mentality, and operated as if they were addressing this issue in a vacuum, rarely consulting either female bishops in other parts of the Anglican Communion or women who exercised oversight in other denominations in Britain, such as the Methodist and Baptist churches.

The Church of England will almost certainly have female bishops by the end of the second decade of this century, but the question has long been: On what terms? Will it be on the same terms as male bishops or not? Will General Synod pass what has become known as a "single clause measure"? That is, will Synod pass straightforward legislation for the ordination and consecration of women as bishops, on equal terms with male bishops, without legally enshrined caveats that discriminate against their ministry?

Looking Forward

General Synod's rejection of legislation for women bishops by six votes in the House of Laity in November 2012 changed everything. It shocked many in the church into the belated realization that

---

15 See especially what became known as the Rochester and Guildford reports, after the bishops who chaired the working parties that produced them, of 2004 and 2006: *Women Bishops in the Church of England? A Report of the House of Bishops' Working Party on Women in the Episcopate* (London: Church House Publishing, 2004) and *Women in the Episcopate: The Guildford Group Report* (London: Church House Publishing, 2006).

prevarication about this was hampering mission and contributing to the church's decline in credibility. It radicalized a younger generation of female priests who were ordained long after the 1992 Act of Synod had been passed. As Brunel University chaplain, the Rev. Sally Hitchiner, put it in describing the debate and the vote, "I was there, I felt like the oxygen was being sucked out of the room as the afternoon wore on and the debate became less and less the inclusive institution I recognized from day-to-day life. I was ordained in the second wave of women priests, the ones who didn't have to fight their way through, I wasn't used to this."[16] Ecclesiastical feminism became more public, or at least there was more awareness of it in the press; people realized that unity at any price was not all right if it was at the expense of women. For those outside the church, the shock was that the church could vote against something so uncontroversial in a world of talented and experienced judges and professors and CEOs who happened to be women. The shock for most inside the church was that this was already a compromised proposal, chock-full of concessions to the small minority of opponents who still rejected it.

The November 2012 vote happened at just the moment when there was a transfer of power at the center, as Rowan Williams stepped down as archbishop of Canterbury and Justin Welby took his place. It was clear to the incoming Archbishop Welby that sorting this out had to be a priority.

All of this meant that when the subject was debated again at General Synod a year later, in November 2013, everyone knew that there could be no failure this time. Justin Welby seemed to have the political will to drive it, and also to bring a group of senior women into the House of Bishops for the interim period, until women are consecrated as bishops and present in their own right. By October 2013, a group of eight senior women had been elected by the regions to attend House of Bishops meetings.[17] This will help to break down the male club atmosphere of the House of Bishops in preparation for the time when women are appointed to the episcopate.

In November 2013, General Synod met and debated a set of guiding principles by which women might be consecrated as bishops.

---

16 http://www.politics.co.uk/comment-analysis/2013/11/21/how-long-can-the-laity-hold-the-church-of-england-ransom-on.

17 http://www.churchofengland.org/media-centre/news/2013/10/final-list-of-female-representatives-to-house-of-bishops.aspx.

This legislative package was passed by an overwhelming majority of 378 votes to 8, with 25 abstentions. This was not legislation for women bishops; it was simply a set of standards by which such legislation would be prepared, and it was remarkably free of the compromises that had dogged all previous proposals. In place of many of those compromises was the more informal idea of an ombudsman, who would be able to sort out any disputes over arrangements for those opposed to female bishops once women are in the episcopate. The *Church Times*, the main Anglican newspaper in England, reported the remarkably friendly and warm expressions from all sides after the proposal passed and noted that the prime minister had said that the government was "ready to work with the Church to see how we can get women bishops into the House of Lords as soon as possible."[18] Many attributed the all-around warmth to the ways in which representatives from all sides had been encouraged to work together on this proposal, and the person behind that was seen to be Archbishop Justin Welby, drawing on his background in conflict resolution and reconciliation (especially in his time as a canon of Coventry Cathedral) and urging people to talk with each other in a way they had not before.

Legislation will be brought to General Synod in 2014. We will wait and see if it passes.

What I hope for the Church of England is that it can get past these internal squabbles about women and indeed about sexuality, and that it can get on with the real work of ministry and mission in a society of few churchgoers alongside many who have a largely unarticulated interest in, and yet a clear thirst for, the spiritual. I hope the Church can stop being inward looking and reach out to new constituencies through multiple different pathways, to demonstrate God's love and a sense of the transcendent. I hope it can do all this with women and men, lay and ordained, working alongside each other on equal terms. I hope it can do this with great effectiveness because it will finally be able to appoint its ministers in terms of gifts and experience, not gender or sexuality or any other external factor such as race or class, drawing on the wisdom of all, so that the work of the gospel may flourish.

---

18 http://www.churchtimes.co.uk/articles/2013/29-november/news/uk/warmth-on-women-bishops.

JANE SHAW is the dean of Grace Cathedral in San Francisco, a position she has held since 2010. Prior to that move, she was dean of divinity and fellow of New College, Oxford, and she taught theology and history at Oxford University for sixteen years. During that time she simultaneously held a variety of other positions: as canon theologian of Salisbury Cathedral; honorary canon of Christ Church Cathedral, Oxford; and theological adviser to the Church of England House of Bishops. She is the author of *Miracles in Enlightenment England* (Yale University Press, 2006); *Octavia, Daughter of God: The Story of a Female Messiah and her Followers* (Yale University Press, 2011); and *A Practical Christianity* (Morehouse Publications, 2012).

CHAPTER 6

Forty Years Later, a Theological Reading

Lauren F. Winner

In 1975, Morehouse Barlow Company brought out a bracing volume of essays called *The Ordination of Women: Pro and Con*.[1] The authors who contributed to the volume included Daniel Corrigan (one of the bishops who participated in the 1974 "irregular" ordination of women) and Suzanne R. Hiatt (one of the "Philadelphia Eleven"). Also numbered in the volume was a priest who chose to write under a pseudonym, David R. Stuart. Stuart's piece was entitled "My Objections to Ordaining Women"; presumably he chose a nom de plume because he judged the position already unfavorable, and was fearful that there might be personal or professional consequences for airing his view. ("[T]he topic is dangerous," "Stuart" wrote at the outset of the essay, "for anyone who ventures to speak out against a popular movement is in personal danger, the danger of being misunderstood and misrepresented, of losing one's privacy and the humility that is more easily maintained in quiet service rather than public debate.") But Stuart's courage, or lack thereof, is not what preoccupies me in this essay. My preoccupation is the argument Stuart made, specifically an argument about women's bodies, about pregnancy, and about sexual desire.

---

1 The volume was edited by Michael P. Hamilton and Nancy S. Montgomery. The most easily accessible edition of the book is online: http://www.womenpriests.org/classic/pc_cont.asp. My quotations are drawn from that edition.

For *The Ordination of Women*, Stanley Atkins, then bishop of Eau Claire, wrote the essay on the "theological case" against women's ordination. His essay argues that in the Bible, ministry is by and large undertaken by men; that "Jesus' choice of men for his apostles is congruous with the masculine imagery used in scripture, and with the historical incarnation of Jesus Christ"; and that the 2,000-year tradition of the church ought not be "set aside lightly." Because Atkins had addressed these "theological" concerns, Stuart was explicitly charged with discussing "the non-theological objections to ordaining women." He divides his ostensibly non-theological arguments into three categories: first the psychological, then the sociological, and, finally, the ecclesiastical.[2] What I wish to suggest in this essay is not that female priests have shown us that Stuart's arguments are specious (although I think that's so), but that female priests have shown us that Stuart's arguments are theological.

★   ★   ★   ★

My chief interest is in the argument Stuart terms "psychological," but I will briefly summarize his "ecclesiastical" and "sociological" arguments. The "ecclesiastical" argument is two-fold: first, the examples of other denominations (Presbyterians, Methodists) that ordain women show that women pastors are a failed experiment, because, for the most part, laypeople don't want women as their clergy. The laypeople who want male pastors, Stuart suggests, are carrying a message of the Paraclete. In some denominations, a perceived call to ministry is self-authenticating, but in Anglican ecclesiology, a call requires corporate discernment, and if laypeople do not want women in the pulpit, then, tautologically, women are not called. Stuart then goes on to suggest that the manner in which women's ordinations had proceeded do not inspire confidence: "Charges, trials, illegal celebrations,

---

2 In this way, Stuart's whole project problematically divides the "theological" from the embodied and relational, a division that runs afoul of any robust doctrine of Incarnation. The very division of sociology from theology is predicated on a view of "the tradition" as a block of knowledge transferred from one generation to the next—a view that suggests that to participate in theological conversation, women need to address *only* their ability to transfer tradition faithfully. The division itself imagines falsely that people's bodies, sexuality, and sociology are not at play every time people pray, preach, pastor, etc. See Kathryn Tanner's reflections on "tradition": Tanner, *Theories of Culture: A New Agenda for Theology* (Minneapolis: Fortress Press, 1997), 134, passim. I am grateful to Amy Laura Hall for her comments on this essay, especially on this point.

angry recriminations—is this chaos to be understood as God the Holy Spirit working his good will among us?" In the service of polemics, this description of the process that led to women's ordination omitted a great deal of decidedly non-chaotic actions: the opening of some Episcopal seminaries to female students in the 1950s, the 1970 vote of the Episcopal Church Women urging women's ordination, and the 1971 vote of the House of Bishops endorsing the same. The problem with Stuart's polemical shorthand is not that it is selective, but that it undercuts his point, for in narrating women's ordination as a story of "charges" and "trials," Stuart has set women's ordination in the narrative frame of Christ's own ministry, a ministry that reached its culmination precisely through charges and a trial. Four decades later, Stuart's polemics suggest, to my ear, not the absence of the Holy Spirit; rather, they suggest Christlikeness. To cast women's ordination as a story of charges and trials is to cast it as a story of Christoformity.[3]

Stuart also makes an argument that he terms "sociological," although it may better be understood as a political argument (insofar as it is about arranging power) masquerading in the language of biology ("The unique glory of a woman is that she is capable of conceiving, gestating, and giving birth to another human being."). Because women give birth and are thus better caregivers than men, church and society must ask: "Do we really want to impose on married women the onerous, around-the-clock and around-the-year demands of a parish priest? I would argue that such a role is in conflict with the best interests of motherhood, probably with that of the baby, and often with that of the congregation." Of course, there are sociological questions here—to this day, sociologists study the intersection of family and the workplace, investigating, among other things, how female clergy have managed the two sets of demands Stuart names, and debating the social and economic structures needed to ensure the flourishing of professional women and their children. But Stuart's sociology has theological problems. Simply put, Christian reasoning can never be grounded in the logic *women have the babies,*

---

3 I have learned the concept of Christoformity from Sarah Jobe, who developed the idea in a series of lectures for Amy Laura Hall's fall 2009 course "Sex, Gender and Discipleship," Duke Divinity School, Durham, North Carolina. Of course, charges and trials are not the only way one can be Christoform. Christoformity can also involve enjoying a wedding party, loving one's friends, or teaching—but another key way to live in a Christlike manner is to find yourself persecuted for witnessing to the truth that God has given you.

therefore... for at least two reasons. First, a focus on women's child-bearing obscures the Christian story's displacement, through baptism, of biological normativity, and its replacement with adoption as a framework for Christian ethics. Second, and perhaps more apposite to conversations about women's participation in the priesthood of Jesus Christ, the assertion that women have babies runs into the problem of Jesus, who is named repeatedly in the Christian tradition as the One who gives birth, and the One who, through nursing, sustains his children. To wit, Anselm, who named Jesus as a mother who gave "birth to me when you made me a Christian." Or the description of Ephrem of Syria: "He was lofty but he sucked Mary's milk, and from His blessings all creation sucks...As indeed He sucked Mary's milk, He has given suck—life to the universe. And again He dwelt in His mother's womb, in His womb dwells all creation." Or Marguerite de Oingt's ode: "The mother who bore me labored for perhaps a day to give me birth, or for a night, while you, lovely, sweet lord, suffered pain because of me not for a night or a day, but rather were in labor for more than thirty years. Ah, love, sweet lord how you must have suffered, your labor was so painful that your holy sweat was like drops of blood which ran over your body and down to the ground." If Jesus is the icon of motherhood, motherhood cannot be a basis for arguing that women cannot be priestly icons of Christ.[4]

★   ★   ★

A woman in the pulpit, dressed in liturgical vestments, cele-brating the Eucharist, and preaching the word to a congregation, threatens the very foundation of patriarchal order; but perhaps more significantly such a woman exposes sexuality in a manner that cannot be denied or disregarded. —Elaine J. Lawless[5]

★   ★   ★

---

4 I develop this argument further in "Interceding: Standing, Kneeling, and Gender," in Stanley Hauerwas and Samuel Wells, eds., *The Blackwell Companion to Christian Ethics*, second edition, (Malden: Blackwell, 2011), 270–271. For Marguerite de Oingt and Anslem, see Caroline Walker Bynum, *Jesus as Mother: Studies in the Spirituality of the High Middle Ages* (Berkeley: University of California Press, 1982), 153, 114. For Ephrem, *Hymns*, trans, Kathleen E. McVey (Mahwah: Paulist Press, 1989), 100.

5 Elaine J. Lawless, *Holy Women, Wholly Women: Sharing Ministries of Wholeness Through Life Stories and Reciprocal Ethnography* (Philadelphia: University of Pennsylvania Press, 1993), 217.

Of Stuart's three arguments, it is the "psychological" that, on my reading, is the most theologically suggestive. The crux of his argument is that "Men were and continue to be the leaders, the initiators, the heads of households familial and ecclesiastical and it would be psychologically confusing as well as historically disruptive to substitute women for that office." Then Stuart offers an elaboration of this claim:

> Reflect for a moment, putting aside those canons of good taste which normally and rightfully govern our thoughts regarding worship, how would you react to the appearance of a pregnant woman in the pulpit? Giving absolution? How would you, the reader—male or female—react to the sight of a beautiful long-haired woman celebrating the Eucharist? Attractive, yes, but also distracting. And I do not believe that the reverse is true, that a handsome male priest produces sexual distractions in the minds of women, for the dynamics of sexual attractiveness work differently for each sex. A handsome young male priest might well elicit feelings of admiration and even love in some women, but it would seldom be inclusive of the sexual phantasies which, for physiological and psychological reasons, occur in a man placed in a similar position vis-à-vis a woman.

From the distance of four decades, there are many things we might like to say in response to Stuart. We might wonder about Stuart's own preoccupations—just what is he revealing about himself in these "psychological" musings? We might like to disabuse him of the notion that straight women are essentially asexual, and might not be turned on by a good-looking man in the altar. But what I want to challenge is his characterization of these assertions as merely psychological, and not also theological.

Indeed, Stuart himself seems to realize he is making a theological argument—his diction, his naming the rules of "good taste" as "canons," suggest it. This may be a "psychological" argument, but it is an argument operating on the semantic terrain of the church. After taking us into that ecclesial semantic field, Stuart places his argument on the backs of two decidedly theological figures: the pregnant woman in the pulpit, and the beautiful woman at the altar. Perhaps before such women were regular features of pulpit- and altar-space, it was easy to imagine that they were "psychological," not theological, figures, but the very women Stuart conjured have showed us precisely how theological their bodies are. One fruit of women's ordination is our much greater capacity to see the theological scaffolding on which Stuart's ruminations sit. One fruit of women's ordination is that we can now more easily see that Stuart is not only writing about men and women; when he invokes pregnant women and beautiful women, he is also writing about God.

Let us start with the pregnant woman in the pulpit. The thing Stuart bids us imagine—he was summoning an absurdity, and a monster—is now an unremarkable sight in many Episcopal churches. (Indeed, in a few short decades, she has become such a fixture of our homiletical imagination as to be almost a cliché of Advent preaching, so much so that I feel compelled to offer the students in my "Women in Ministry" class two cautionary reminders: first, there are other Advent sermons they can preach than the sermon that invokes their own pregnancies; and second, there are other moments in the Christian story besides Mary's first Advent that their pregnant bodies might illumine.)

Preachers and pastors who are or have been pregnant have drawn on pregnancy to teach us, *inter alia*, about Lenten wilderness[6]; about the ways that we are all called to participate in the birthing of God's kingdom[7]; about prayer[8]; and about the reign of God.[9] But it is not just the sermons preached by (and the books written by) pregnant clergywomen that are teaching us. It is also their very bodies. Pregnant women have helped me understand what Jesus might have meant when he said "Abide in me, and I will abide in you." As Baptist pastor Sarah Jobe has written, "We don't have lots of examples" of people abiding in one another. In fact, "Pregnancy is perhaps the best example we have of one person welcoming another into her body the

---

6 Teresa Delgado, "Calling All Wild Women: Reflections on the Wilderness, Luke 4:1–13" in Lee Hancock, ed., *The Book of Women's Sermons: Hearing God in Each Other's Voices* (Maryknoll: Orbis Books, 1999), 86–90.

7 Meredith Stone, "Preaching Pregnant in Advent," http://ministryandmotherhood. com/2013/12/18/meredith-stone-preaching-pregnant-in-advent/

8 Stephanie Paulsell, *Honoring the Body: Meditations on a Christian Practice* (San Francisco: Jossey-Bass, 2002), 69–70.

9 Julie Cadwallader-Staub, "Pregnancy and the Reign of God." *Sarah's Daughters*, 12.1 (Jan–Feb. 1986), 10.

way Jesus asks us to live in him." Jesus' promise "Abide in me, and I will abide in you," sounds bizarre, notes Jobe. It sounds like a koan, hard to grasp, hard even to ponder. And yet, "pregnant women and [their] babies do it every day." Pregnancy also teaches us about the Eucharist. Pregnant women's bodies can show us how to hear Jesus' assertion that his body is real food (John 6:55)—the bodies of pregnant women, after all, are the only bodies around that will automatically give calcium from their own bones to sustain someone else's body. Stuart asks how I "react to the appearance of a pregnant woman in the pulpit." I react with thanksgiving, because the figure of the pregnant preacher is a theological figure. Perhaps more than any other bodies in church, her body shows forth the image of Christ.[10]

What about those canons of good taste? To be sure, there is still, in our society, some discomfort around pregnancy. But, whatever our squeamishness in talking about pregnancy and assigning pregnancy theological weight, to speak of the pregnancy as theological is easier than speaking of the beautiful female body, the sexy female body, as carrying theological meaning. Forty years after Stuart wrote, the church is managing to give language to what we can learn from pregnancy—maternity feels both benign and dangerous, approachable and unapproachable with theological rhetoric. "Distracting" female beauty does not have the same sentimentalized safety. Female beauty is only frightening, only unsettling.

The beautiful female body, the disruptingly erotic female body, is also a theological body. Consider what Emily Wachner had to say to my aforementioned students in the spring of 2014. Wachner is a priest on staff at Trinity Wall Street, and is also well-known for her turn on the TV show *What Not To Wear* (in each episode, a pair of New York fashionistas give an unsuspecting person a wardrobe makeover). Wachner generously offered to Skype into my class for our discussion of clerical clothing; of the many wise things she said, I was most struck by her reminder that a clergywoman's sartorial choices convey something important to the women in the congregation. Specifically, clergywomen's clothing shape female parishioners' understandings of what is acceptable for "Christian women": female priests' garb helps set the terrain on which other women imagine

---

10 Sarah Jobe, *Creating with God: The Holy Confusing Blessedness of Pregnancy* (Brewster: Paraclete Press, 2011), 91–118.

Christian womanhood. So Wachner sometimes wears ankle boots with zippers on Sunday morning. She does this because everything that is on the altar is good, and beloved of God, accepted by God, and Wachner wants the women in her congregation to know that women's sexuality is part of that goodness, that belovedness, that acceptance. There's no real way to look sexy in an alb, said Wachner. She is very beautiful, but no one is going to look at her in her alb and mistake it for a negligee. But they might see those boots and imagine, or remember, that whatever else Wachner is, she is also sexual. And that imagining, pace Stuart, is precisely not alien to the altar; it is precisely not other than what the altar is about.

In our society, it may be that women are uniquely equipped to carry sexuality to the altar and to remind us that it is part of what is good, beloved, accepted. As Elaine J. Lawless has written about clergymen, "The Protestant minister, unlike the priest, can marry and his wife can bear his children. So he has never been involved in the pretense of clerical asexuality. Even so, his sexual nature is shielded. In the pulpit he may stand in vestments or in a business suit; he may be adored by some women in the congregation; he may even be the subject of cruel innuendo or scandalous stories. But whatever the congregation whispers, the minister does not *signify* sexuality."[11] Perhaps this is an instance of "what man intended for evil, God worked for good"—because women's bodies have been so hyper-sexualized, women's bodies at the altar are able to show us that sexuality is beloved of God.

★   ★   ★   ★   ★

The women Stuart conjures—pretty women, pregnant women (dare we even imagine they are one in the same, the distractingly pretty, erotically alluring, seven-month-pregnant woman?) in pulpits and altars—are increasingly familiar sights. And still they are threatening.

What is the threat? The threat is to our ways of ordering society. The threat is to how we distribute power. And the threat is also, perhaps most elementally, to how we image God.[12] But Scripture has already told us that God is a pregnant woman—does not Isaiah 42:14

---

11 Lawless, 219.
12 Lawless, 220–221, and passim.

tell us that? And Scripture already tells us that God has a beauty to which we are erotically drawn—does not the Transfiguration tell us that?[13] The Scriptures already provide answers to Stuart's rhetorical questions. But female priests are good to read with. Female priests are signs. Pregnant priests, beautiful priests, disruptive and distracting bodies, witness to God.

It is now 40 years after Stuart wrote. I assign his essay to my students and they find it insulting, and silly, and discomfiting, and absurd. I hope that 40 years from now, someone reads this essay, and finds it as stupefying as my students find Stuart's. I hope readers in 40 years find my need to argue for the theological significations of women's bodies curious—curious because that theological significance is so obvious as to require no arguing. And I hope those readers find my suggestion that it is hard to talk about alluring female bodies at the altar, insulting, and silly, and discomfiting, and absurd.

LAUREN WINNER is Assistant Professor of Christian Spirituality at Duke Divinity School and author, most recently, of "Still: Notes on a Mid-Faith Crisis." Ordained to the priesthood in 2011, she serves St. Paul's Episcopal Church in Louisburg, NC, and a member of the board of the Episcopal Preaching Foundation. Dr. Winner holds degrees from Clare College, Cambridge, Duke Divinity School, and Columbia University.

---

13 I owe my appreciation of the erotic dimension of the Transfiguration to Graham Ward's marvelous essay "Bodies: The Displaced Body of Jesus Christ," in John Milbank, Catherine Pickstock, and Graham Ward, eds., *Radical Orthodoxy: A New Theology* (London: Routledge, 1999), 163–181.

CHAPTER 7

The Ordination of Women: Some Theological Implications

Marilyn McCord Adams

The question "How has the theology of The Episcopal Church (TEC) changed with the ordination of women?" is ambiguous. It could be asking what most members of TEC actually believe, in which case it would best be answered by survey-taking social scientists. The results might be surprising, because TEC is notorious for its lack of interest in gate-keeping. We have doctrinal norms, most notably the historic creeds that we recite in the daily offices and in the Eucharist. Baptismal candidates answer "yes" to the interrogatory version of the Apostles' Creed,[1] and clergy swear an ordination oath to uphold TEC's doctrines, disciplines, and worship.[2] But—once these rites of initiation are over—TEC shows a principled aversion to checking up on whether even leaders among its members are toeing the doctrinal line. The reason is that TEC expects its members to *grow* in the knowledge and love of God as revealed in Jesus Christ. Every spiritual director knows: growth is a messy process, with ups and downs, doubts and deviations, before it delivers a person into new levels of maturity.

---

1 The Book of Common Prayer and Administration of the Sacraments and Other Rites and Ceremonies of the Church Together with the Psalter or Psalms of David According to the Use of the Episcopal Church (New York: Church Hymnal Corporation, 1979), 304.
2 Book of Common Prayer, 518, 526, 538.

TEC means to house this whole development. Orthodoxy tests would confuse TEC's message: "Come and stay through the chances and changes of life! We are a church for all seasons!"

Happily for me, since I am a theologian and not a social scientist, there is another way of reading the question. TEC's decisions over the last forty years to open the ordination process to women and LGBT persons and to authorize rites for blessing same-sex couples, have changed institutional sex-and-gender policies in ways that many Anglicans have found disturbing. One fruit of the resulting controversies has been to make some theological implications of TEC's institutional policy changes explicit. In what follows, I want to comment on four that have to do with ecclesial norms and holy orders.

The Strong Argument from Tradition

First, TEC's decision to ordain women and coupled LGBT persons implies *a rejection of the strong argument from tradition*. The argument from tradition makes what was believed and practiced traditionally a *weighty* consideration in debates about what the institutional church should profess and practice now. Many Anglicans have taken "tradition" to refer to what the undivided church believed and practiced before the schism between East and West, while Roman Catholics often give tradition a longer run. Certainly, TEC pays its respects to tradition in many ways. The Lambeth Quadrilateral forwards the historic Apostles' and Nicene Creeds as norms of faith. Not only ordinands, but EFM students are required to study patristic theology. TEC's Book of Common Prayer not only scripts the regular recitation of the historic creeds; its Eucharistic prayers participate in the revival of patristic liturgy. TEC's prayer book also includes a series of historical documents that have loomed large in Christian reflection and Anglican formation.

TEC insists that its clergy and encourages its members to take traditional theology very seriously. At every prayer book service, TEC gives voice to ancient prayers. But TEC does not take traditional thought and practice to be *decisive* the way the Roman Catholic and the Eastern Orthodox Churches do. Not all aspects of church life are equally important. But *the strong argument from tradition says that—where essentials are concerned—if tradition never permitted it, that settles it!* For Roman Catholic and Eastern Orthodox Churches, the very existence of the church depends on divinely legitimated sacramental ministers. Because they read tradition as persistently for-bidding the ordination of women, they conclude that they are "not free" to change their institutional policies in this respect.[3]

By contrast, TEC takes for granted a distinction between doc-trinal norms in the historic creeds and ecumenical councils, and eth-ical norms preached and practiced down through the ages. This fact became salient in the church court's 1995 decision in response to the presentment against Bishop Walter Righter. The basic outline of salvation history, the fundamental understandings of God as triune and incarnate formulated in the patristic period, are points that TEC takes Scripture and tradition to have settled. But where ethical norms are concerned, TEC expects the church to keep growing in its grasp of God's vision of the ideal society, of what it is to love God and neighbor. This is because TEC recognizes that the human race is socially challenged, neither smart enough nor good enough to orga-nize utopia. Human social arrangements always spawn systemic evils, structures of cruelty that privilege some by degrading others. Because we do not understand the properties of systems very well, and because we have such a stake in social stability, it is possible for those who benefit most from society to go for centuries without even noticing such evils, much less appreciating what is so bad about them. Think of how long it has taken the human race to recognize slavery as an abomination to the Lord! Moreover, human beings have a natural tendency to think that God agrees with, even sponsors and enforces, the norms needed to maintain our society. To let tradition be decisive in setting practice risks perpetuating the systemic evils of ages past. TEC insists, on the contrary, that it is our Christian duty to uproot them. That is why it has acted to remove race, ethnic origin, gender, and sexual orientation as barriers to consideration for ordination.[4]

Arguments from Ecumenical Consensus

Second, TEC'S sex-and-gender institutional policy changes imply *a rejection of arguments from ecumenical consensus* that—where essentials

---

3 See The Archbishops' Council, *Women in the Episcopate? An Anglican-Roman Catholic Dialogue* (London: 2008); and The Anglican Consultative Council, *The Church of the Triune God: The Cyprus Agreed Statement of the International Commission for Anglican-Orthodox Theological Dialogue 2006* (London: Apollo Print Generation, 2006).

4 See *The Constitutions and Canons of the Episcopal Church,* Title III, Canon 1, sec. 2.

of doctrine and practice are concerned—an ecclesial body should not make changes without the agreement of the church worldwide. In recent Anglican Communion worries about the ordination of women and coupled LGBT persons, this argument came in several versions.[5] Some made it a condition of good standing in the Anglican Communion that a national church not proceed with changes in sex-and-gender policies about whom to ordain and which partnerships to bless, unless and until all member churches agreed to the substance of the new policy. Others allowed that a national church might proceed but should hold the policy change to be provisional unless and until it was "received" by all member churches. Thus, when the Church of England finally did go ahead with the ordination of women, it conceded to conscientious objectors that the change in practice was "under reception" and might be revoked if consensus was not eventually reached. Some arguments strengthened the demand for consensus another way: such policy changes should be subject to the advice and consent, not only of other churches in the Anglican Communion, but also of favored ecumenical discussion partners, most especially, the Roman Catholic and Eastern Orthodox Churches.

Although TEC has shown patience in listening to conscientious objectors at home and abroad, allowed dioceses leeway in implementing the policies, and arranged alternative pastoral oversight for those who cannot in conscience accept the ministry of women or coupled LGBT persons, TEC has proceeded to institute the policy changes and does not regard their force as provisional or dependent on ecumenical consensus. TEC recognizes that the Holy Spirit is busy infiltrating and transforming cultures worldwide. But there are dramatic differences in cultures. While it is important to keep up the conversations and share convictions about what we think the Holy Spirit is doing in our midst, there is also little reason to think that the Holy Spirit starts at the same place in every culture. Much more

---

5 Such arguments are found in *The Virginia Report* (1997), *The Windsor Report* (2004), and the first two draft covenants: *The Nassau Draft Covenant* (2007), sec. 6 (3–6), and *The St. Andrews Draft Covenant* (2008), sec. 1.2.6. Then Archbishop Rowan Williams also forwards such reasoning in his *Challenge and Hope of Being and Anglican Today* (2006), http://rowanwilliams.archbishopofcanterbury. org/articles.php/1478/the-challenge-and-hope-of-being-an-anglican-today-a-reflection-for-the-bishops-clergy-and-faithful-o and *The Archbishop of Canterbury's Advent Letter* (2007), http://www.anglicannews.org/news/2007/12/archbishop-of-canterburys-advent-letter.aspx

plausible is that the Holy Spirit pioneers one transformation here and another there, depending on where people were readiest to move. The argument from ecumenical consensus threatens to quench the Spirit. TEC insists that our calling is to discern for all we're worth and then live up to the light that is in us, trusting God to make good on our mistakes.

Infallible Plain-Sense Hermeneutics

Third, TEC's changes in sex-and-gender policies imply *a rejection of the infallible authority of plain-sense readings of Scripture*. In the Church of England, conservative evangelical groups argue that the Bible forbids women to have authority over men and demands that women keep silent in the church, and that settles it! They also reason that every mention of homosexual intercourse in the Bible condemns it, and that settles it! In recent Anglican Communion disputes, conservative evangelicals tried to write these verdicts into early drafts of the proposed Anglican Covenant by requiring that member churches all adhere to "biblical morality." Covenant-drafters also tried to reassert the binding authority of the Thirty-Nine Articles of Religion over member churches, because Article XX decrees that "it is not lawful for the Church to ordain any thing that is contrary to God's Word written, neither may it so expound one place of Scripture, that it be repugnant to another."[6] They take this to imply that plain-sense harmonizing is the hermeneutic of choice.

TEC is unequivocal about the Bible as a primary authority for Christian belief and practice. The ordination oath required of all TEC clergy reads: "I solemnly declare that I do believe the Holy Scriptures of the Old and New Testaments to be the Word of God, and to contain all things necessary for salvation."[7] Until the 1984 Alternative Service Book, clergy in the Church of England were required to subscribe to the Thirty-Nine Articles. TEC's bishops, priests, and deacons are not. TEC's prayer book recognizes the Thirty-Nine Articles not as binding but as historical documents significant for the self-definition of the Church of England and reflecting distinctive theological controversies of those times. Doubtless, some TEC clergy hold

---

6 Book of Common Prayer, 871.
7 Book of Common Prayer, 526, 538.

to biblical infallibility on a plain-sense reading. Doubtless, some TEC clergy find that the Thirty-Nine Articles speak for them. TEC tolerates these minority reports as individual convictions, but no longer allows them the institutional expression of barring women and coupled LGBT persons from the ordination process. Individual TEC clergy may refuse to bless, but they can no longer appeal to such convictions to keep other TEC clergy from blessing same-sex couples.

So far, I have been pointing out how TEC's institutional policy changes regarding sex-and-gender have theological implications about *the loci of authority in the church*. The authority of Scripture is primary, but—on plain-sense readings—it is not infallible. Tradition is a secondary authority, to be taken seriously, but it is neither infallible nor decisive for belief and practice. Underlying these conclusions is the conviction that both Scripture and tradition are shaped by the cultures of their human authors, and so may bear the marks of the systemic evils that those cultures spawned. It is not surprising if patriarchy and taboos against homosexuality were deeply imbedded in Bedouin and agrarian Near Eastern cultures and so made their way into Leviticus. Religions are conservative, and so it is unremarkable if such sentiments survived into the first-century rabbinic schools in which St. Paul was formed. But there will be no place for taboos in the reign of God. This is why TEC's policy overrides any notion that biblical and patristic sex-and-gender injunctions should have decisive weight.

Baptism as Chief among Holy Orders

A fourth argument derives from a different source, namely, TEC's refocussing of its doctrine of ministry to emphasize the priesthood of all believers. Historically, Luther and Calvin had championed this fourth order of ministry alongside the ancient three-fold division of holy orders into bishops, priests, and deacons. Early on, however, the Church of England blurred this insight. For in its polemics against Rome, it rested its claim to be a true church on its being governed by bishops in the apostolic succession. The theory was that Christ himself had founded the church and dictated many of its organizational details. In particular, he not only commissioned the apostles to preach the gospel, he endowed them with sacramental faculties, not only to celebrate the Eucharist, but to ordain successor bishops. These successor bishops would be not only guardians of doctrine and discipline, but also the fontal source of reproducing Christians, the only ones empowered to ordain and the ones best suited to confirm and baptize. Only bishops in the apostolic succession would inherit and receive the supernatural powers needed for the continuing life of the church.

The doctrine of apostolic succession was vigorously reasserted in the early twentieth century,[8] when—after flirting with some ecumenical agreement with the Church of England—Rome declared Anglican orders invalid. Once again, Anglican divines retorted, the Church of England is a *real* church, because it has retained bishops in the apostolic succession. The Lambeth Quadrilateral, which was originally formulated as a platform for ecumenical consensus between Protestants and Roman Catholics, includes episcopal government as one of its four planks (the others being Scripture, the historic Apostles' and Nicene Creeds, and the dominical sacraments). This desire to assert legitimacy in the face of Rome and the Eastern Orthodox Churches led for a time to a strident insistence that no ecumenical agreements with Protestant denominations could go forward, unless nonepiscopally ordained clergy agreed to be reordained by a bishop in the apostolic succession. The polemics also hinted that while the episcopate and "ministerial priesthood" were essential to the very existence of the church (its *esse* or being, not just its *bene esse* or well-being), the priesthood of all believers was at most relevant to its well-being (the *bene esse*, not the *esse*).

Such clericalism had been reinforced in medieval theology by the belief that the sacramental rites of the church conferred supernatural qualities or powers and so involved what came to be called "an ontological change." For example, Aquinas explains that baptism confers the "baptismal character," a supernatural passive power that makes a person eligible to participate in worship and receive further grace thereby. Confirmation adds supernatural power that would strengthen the believer to make a bold confession under adverse circumstances. Ordination confers an indelible character, active power to perform rites that make supernatural graces available to others. Ordained

---

8 See Charles Gore, *The Church and Ministry* (London: Longmans, Green & Co., 1919); and Dom Gregory Dix, "The Ministry in the Early Church c. A.D. 90–410," in *The Apostolic Ministry: Essays on the History and Doctrine of Episcopacy,* ed. Kenneth E. Kirk (London: Hodder & Stoughton, 1946), 185–303.

ministers had extra and extra-special supernatural powers that the merely baptized and confirmed did not share. Aquinas thought that—given the way that Christ has chosen to organize the church—the ordained ministry was essential to the reproduction of new Christians, and the episcopate was necessary to the reproduction of new priests.[9]

The strong argument from tradition led medievals to a further claim: if male and female alike can receive the supernatural characters conferred by baptism and confirmation, ordination is reserved for males. However much a bishop might intone the prayers and lay on hands, it wouldn't "take" with women. No supernatural character would be infused into her, and no sacramental graces would flow to the faithful when she performed sacramental rites. Duns Scotus recognized the oddity of this, given that ordination bestows such spiritual benefits, given that men and women share a common human nature, and given that women often possess extraordinary leadership abilities. He reasoned that if this exclusion of women from ordained ministry were of merely human origin, it would be unjust. The strong argument from tradition weighed in to lead him to the remarkable conclusion that the restriction of ordination to men must have come directly from Christ himself![10]

About the same time as TEC was coming to accept the ordination of women, it was also drawing the conclusion that the traditional ministerial pyramid needed to be turned upside down. Instead of putting bishops at the apex, priests a little lower, deacons lower still, with the laity at the base, the priesthood of all believers should top the pyramid, while the ministries of deacons, priests, and bishops should be derivative and so descend from that as variations on a theme. For this contention, there was a theological rationale. Ministry is not merely a matter of performing a function in humanly devised institutions. Tradition is right: ministry involves something supernatural. Baptism is the principal holy order, because in baptism the Holy Spirit comes to dwell in the hearts of the baptized. All Christians are called to lifelong collaboration with the Holy Spirit to spread the Good News of God's love in the world. This supranatural gift of indwelling Holy Spirit is what is necessary for the existence (*esse*) of the church. Collaboration with the Holy Spirit in

---

9 Aquinas, *Summa Theologica* III, qq.63, 65, 72.

10 John Duns Scotus, *Reportata Parisiensia* IV, d.25, q.2, nn.5–9; Wadding XI.2.784–85.

ministry by *all* of its members is necessary to the flourishing (the *bene esse*) of the church. Accordingly, TEC's *Constitutions and Canons* open the section on "Ministry" with a discussion of the ministry of the baptized,[11] which is then followed by treatments of the roles of bishop, priest, and deacon.[12]

Of course, traditionalists would agree that there is a sense in which baptism is the principal holy order: baptism initiates persons into church membership, makes them members of the body of Christ, which is a necessary condition of leading any sort of Christian life. The view of traditionalists was and is that necessary conditions are not sufficient conditions. *Only* the baptized are eligible to be considered for ordination, but—they insist—*not all* of the baptized are eligible to be considered for ordination as bishops, priests, and deacons. Traditionalists maintain that there are other necessary conditions, including that the persons be male and that they not be coupled homosexuals. Roman Catholics add that bishops and priests must be unmarried (Rome has lately come to ordain married men to the diaconate). Eastern Orthodox Churches require that if the future priest is to marry, it must be prior to ordination. In the Church of England, there is a lingering hesitation to consecrate persons as bishops if they are divorced and remarried and/or if they are married to someone who has divorced, where the former spouse is still alive.

Advocates of the ordination of women and coupled homosexuals countered with the chant: *"If you won't ordain us, don't baptize us!"* In pressing this sentiment, they were not confusing necessary and sufficient conditions, but forwarding *a strong doctrine of baptism.*[13] All agree, baptism confers the Holy Spirit and makes us members of Christ's body. The strong doctrine of baptism goes further: baptism washes away traditional impediments to being considered for ordained ministry in the church. TEC's canons make it explicit: race, national origin, ethnicity, gender, sexual orientation, marital status, and some disabilities are not sufficient disqualifying conditions.[14] *TEC's institutional posture implies that the church thought so, only because it was gripped by the systemic evils of the societies of which it was a part.*

---

11 *Constitutions and Canons*, Title III, Canon 1.
12 *Constitutions and Canons*, Title III, Canons 6–12.
13 I thank the Reverend Lisa Fischbeck and the Reverend Shawnthea Monroe for bringing me to clarity on this point.
14 *Constitutions and Canons*, Title III, Canon 1, sec.2.

The strong doctrine of baptism is radical and bears repeating. What is key is membership in Christ's body and the gift of indwelling Holy Spirit. What follows is a life partnership of long-term and day-to-day discernment of what the baptized and the Holy Spirit will do together, both individually and in community. The variety of gifts and the distinctiveness of human personalities mean that different habits of collaboration (if you like, "supernatural characters") will be built up in different persons. "Different strokes for different folks!" When we are working with the Holy Spirit, why suppose that grace comes in standardized "one size fits all" packages when intimate acquaintance and divine resourcefulness could produce the tailor-made?

This last rhetorical question invites us to go beyond Anglican traditions, the Lambeth Quadrilateral, and TEC's current canons to wonder whether the three-fold ordained ministry of bishops, priests, and deacons is not a historical artifact, whether it does not represent an abstraction and condensation into roles of what are in principle aspects of the ministries of all Christians. If history and experience make us doubt that Christ dictated the organizational details of the church once and for all time, we might think instead that institutional structures are skillful means that should not be allowed to outlive their usefulness for every long. Flirting further with this strong doctrine of baptism might be just what is needed to restructure the church to move forward into the future.

MARILYN MCCORD ADAMS is a theologian and Episcopal priest who specializes in historical and philosophical theology. Ordained in Hollywood during the 80s AIDS epidemic, she has been an LGBT activist ever since. She has taught at a number of schools, including UCLA, Yale Divinity School, and Oxford University, where she was the first woman (and first American) Regius Professor of Divinity and member of the General Synod of the Church of England during Communion-wide controversies about ordaining LGBT and blessing LGBT partnerships. Her "medieval" books include *William Ockham; What Sort of Human Nature?: Medieval Philosophy and Systematics of Christology;* and *Some Late Medieval Theories of the Eucharist.* She has also authored two books on the problem of suffering: *Horrendous Evils and the Goodness of God* and *Christ and Horrors: The Coherence of Christology.* In addition, she has published a book of sermons, *Wrestling for Blessing,* and a book of prayers, *Opening to God: Childlike Prayers for Adults.*

Chapter 8

"Stand There and Be a Woman": Women in the House of Deputies

Gay Clark Jennings

I find it poor logic to say that because women are good, women should vote. Men do not vote because they are good; they vote because they are male, and women should vote, not because we are angels and men are animals, but because we are human beings and citizens of this country.
—Winona Ryder as Jo March, *Little Women* (1994)

Living with the Legacy

It's been a long century. The Episcopal Church began discussing whether to seat women in the House of Deputies in 1913, and we didn't get the job done until 1970. Twenty-one years after that, in 1991, Pamela Chinnis became the first woman elected as president of the House of Deputies, and in 2012, I became the first ordained woman elected to that post.

During this long century, some of us women have come a long way. There's no doubt that including female leaders, lay and ordained, has changed the church, the way we govern ourselves, and the way we understand broader issues of inclusion. The movement for women's leadership established networks, generated momentum, and raised up leaders who pushed for the full inclusion of gay, lesbian, bisexual, and transgender people in the life of the church and galvanized other movements for social justice.

In turn, we have faced theological and political crises brought about by bishops, clergy, and laity leaving the church and challenging our historic polity and system of authority in a bid to take property and money with them. This threat, and the reality of declining resources across the mainline church, have engendered an urge to centralize authority in the church's corporate structure and in the House of Bishops. In many ways, this centralizing impulse is a legacy of the struggle for women's authority. As Pamela Darling wrote nearly twenty years ago:

> Changes in women's roles in the past twenty-five years have challenged the ecclesiastical structures of the Episcopal Church more profoundly than any other social issue in the two centuries since it was first organized in 1789. During that time women moved from near-invisibility within the church's institutional structures into positions in every area of lay and ordained leadership. These dramatic institutional changes placed immense stress on the church's spiritual framework, threatening its traditional interpretations of authority, morality, and theology and demonstrating that the subordination of women had been a necessary element in traditional ecclesiastical structures. Like old wineskins, those structures threatened to burst with the new wine of mutuality between men and women.[1]

The structures haven't ruptured yet, but even forty-four years after the first seating of female deputies and forty years after the first ordinations of women, our ecclesial impulse in times of great change and great stress is to circle the wagons, tighten up the hierarchy, and limit the kinds of leadership we accept and the variety of voices we hear. If we reflect on the extraordinary changes of the last four decades, perhaps we can remember how the church has been strengthened by women's leadership and be bold enough to continue on the path that lies ahead.

---

1 Pamela W. Darling, *New Wine: The Story of Women Transforming Leadership and Power in the Episcopal Church* (Cambridge, MA: Cowley Publications, 1994), 219.

Money Talks to the House of Deputies

The final barriers to women being seated as deputies were finally dissolved by a potent cocktail of grace, shame, and money. But they were immobile for many years. As Pamela Darling writes in *New Wine*:

> Time after time the women of the Triennial politely petitioned, and time after time the deputies refused—as each Convention duly performed the rituals of deference and power embedded in the United Thank Offering, modestly presented by the women and magnanimously received by the men. Power does not bow to deference, and it was not until a greater power was exerted, in the form of the increasingly embarrassing distance between secular and church practices highlighted by Presiding Bishop Lichtenberger's sharp rebuke in 1964, that the men of the Convention finally voted to allow women to join them as deputies.[2]

Lichtenberger, a beloved bishop who was retiring due to ill health, spoke in firm tones to a joint session of the 1964 General Convention, pointing out to the assembled men the contradiction inherent in their refusal to seat women in spite of their willingness to accept nearly $5 million from the United Thank Offering and to adopt a document titled "Mutual Responsibility and Interdependence" from the 1963 Anglican Congress. "What we did this morning and what we do now is reality—the other is, I believe, the unwillingness to face the fact that women are members of the Body of Christ, that they are of the laity and members of the Body of Christ," he said.

Later in the day, House of Deputies President Clifford Morehouse, a distinguished publisher and supporter of seating female deputies, called the house to order and directed that Presiding Bishop Lichtenberger's statement be read again. Despite the appeal, the deputies were unhappy with the presiding bishop's attempt to influence business in the House of Deputies and stood firm.[3]

At the next General Convention, in 1967, the deputies finally gave way. Thanks to the work of the Archives of the Episcopal Church, the story has been preserved for us.[4]

---

2 Darling, *New Wine*, 221.
3 Darling, *New Wine*, 90–91.
4 Lueta Bailey, interview by Mary S. Donovan, August 23, 1983, the Archives of the Episcopal Church; this is also the source for subsequent quotations related to Lueta Bailey.

Five conventions before the historic vote, in 1952, the Woman's Auxiliary, now called the Episcopal Church Women, had asked to become the third House of General Convention. That request, as well as what had by then become a usual resolution to seat women as deputies, was denied. But as the Episcopal Church Women's financial power grew, so did women's political clout. The United Thank Offering, which had totaled just over $44,000 in 1875, was up to $2 million by 1949 and in 1951, received a single donation of over $1 million in addition to smaller gifts and coins dropped into its ubiquitous blue boxes.[5]

At the 1967 General Convention, Lueta Bailey of the Diocese of Atlanta was presiding officer of the Episcopal Church Women's Triennial meeting, and she found herself at the center of a storm. Presiding Bishop John Hines was promoting a $9 million "Special Program" that he said would allow The Episcopal Church to "take its place humbly and boldly alongside of, and in support of, the dispossessed and oppressed peoples of this country for the healing of our national life."

Bailey had been introduced to the issue of seating women female deputies in 1955 at General Convention in Honolulu, when she was first a delegate to the women's Triennial Meeting. "I heard my first debate about women being seated as deputies and walked out because I was so angry I didn't know what to do," she told Dr. Mary Sudman Donovan, herself a pioneer of women's history in The Episcopal Church, in an interview for the Archives of the Episcopal Church in 1983. She was, she said, "in the House of Deputies and could only stand on the outside, you know, looking in . . ."

With Bailey presiding, the Triennial Meeting voted to approve Hines's request that they contribute $3 million to the Special Program. The vote took place before the General Convention considered the matter, and the women's commitment to provide a third of the necessary funding exerted tremendous influence on the debate. Not through canonical change, but through budget, women had begun to exert *de facto* authority in the governance of the church.

This turn of events led some male deputies to complain, forcefully, that the women and their money were exercising too much

---

5 Anne B. Fulk, "Triennial Yesterday . . . The Matrix Affirmed." *Triennial Today* ca. 1991, courtesy of the Archives of the Episcopal Church.

power. "We were constantly—harassment is not a good word but you never walked anywhere that some man who was a deputy didn't bring up the subject," Bailey said. She responded firmly and practically by locking the doors of the Triennial meeting hall. "Some were encouraged but others were not and that's why we kept the doors locked. Because I knew some of those prominent men and they could come in and influence us."

Then came the vote on admitting women as deputies. Bailey and her peers debated whether or not Bailey should go to address the House of Bishops and the House of Deputies if they voted against seating women." My feeling had been yes, I go no matter what. . . . I was not going to be ungracious," she said. "It didn't mean that I had to go in there and say beautiful things to them. I had two speeches."

"I decided early that morning to wear a red silk suit and announce that to the whole Triennial meeting that if they voted no I was dressed properly for the martyr and if they voted yes I was dressed properly for the celebration."

First the House of Deputies and then the House of Bishops voted in favor of seating women as deputies. "As I walked down the aisle [in the House of Deputies] I'll never forget the mass of men snapping pictures of me going down. . . . It was a great day in the life of the church. And it was not Lueta Bailey, it was all the women walking down that aisle." On that day, she became the first woman to address General Convention.

Three years later, at the 1970 General Convention in Houston, women were seated as deputies following a second affirmative vote in both houses. Bailey was among the first group of twenty-nine women seated in the House. The *Journal of the General Convention 1970* tells the parliamentary story:

> The Secretary read Message No. 2 from the House of Bishops, which informed this House that the Bishops had concurred with Deputies' Message No. 2, in adopting, in final action, the amendment of Section 4 of Article 1 of the Constitution, which, by substituting "lay person" for "layman," removes all constitutional barriers to the seating of women as Deputies in the General Convention.[6]

---

6 General Convention, *Journal of the General Convention of . . . The Episcopal Church, Houston,* 1970 (New York: General Convention, 1970), 127.

The president of the House, John Coburn—who went on to become a beloved bishop of Massachusetts—then recognized the chair of the Committee on Elections, who reported that twenty-nine women had been properly certified and were entitled to be seated in the House. "At the invitation of the President," records the *Journal*, "the newly seated women Deputies were escorted to the front of the Chamber by other members of their Deputations. When all were assembled, the President, addressing the House, for the first time, with the words, 'Ladies and gentlemen,' introduced Mrs. Bailey. . . . On behalf of her fellow Deputies, Mrs. Bailey addressed the House, after which the new Deputies took their seats."

Bailey had advocated for marking the seating of the first women deputies with a moment of recognition. "The debate had been so ugly and so long in the church that there had to be a moment of reconciliation. Let's forget all of those bad words, and they had hurt. You know, stand there and be a woman."

In 2010, House of Deputies President Bonnie Anderson, my predecessor, presented Bailey with an award commemorating the fortieth anniversary of the seating of women as deputies.[7]

A Sea of Black Suits, or, Does My Baptism Matter?

My own memory of General Convention picks up six years later, when, as a senior in seminary, I attended the 1976 General Convention. I'd been married for less than two weeks when I left my husband to set up our first apartment and headed to Minneapolis to witness the vote on the ordination of women. I sat in the visitors' bleachers, looking down on a House of Deputies that was still a sea of men dressed in black suits—at that convention, only 16 percent of deputies were women—thinking how strange it was that only men in the House of Bishops, and primarily men in the House of Deputies were voting on whether or not women's baptisms matter.

My thinking had been shaped by the "Report on the Validity of the Philadelphia Ordinations," written by Richard Norris Jr. of General Theological Seminary and three other recognized theologians at the request of the Diocese of Rochester. The report, which

---

7 Jim Naughton, "Lueta Bailey: Woman of Courage and Determination," *Pathways: Quarterly Journal of the Episcopal Diocese of Atlanta* (Winter 2010–2011): 20–21.

was a response to the House of Bishops' determination that the ordinations of the Philadelphia Eleven had not been valid, determined that the ordinations had been "valid but irregular" and asserted that denying ordination to women was "implicitly to deny or qualify the meaning of women's baptism."[8]

In 1976, to this young seminarian, The Episcopal Church was way behind the times. Everywhere in the culture, women were demanding and receiving equality. Ten years earlier, Catherine East and Betty Friedan had formed the National Organization for Women—NOW— and, as Mark Kurlansky details in his book *1968: The Year That Rocked the World*,[9] the group moved quickly to advocate that newspapers stop separating help wanted listings by gender. They made progress with major New York newspapers in 1967, and the U.S. Supreme Court ruled against the practice in 1973. So when even help wanted ads could no longer discriminate against women, how could the church?

The final vote took place in the House of Deputies on September 16, 1976. During the debate, twenty-nine deputies spoke in favor of the resolution, which had already been passed by the House of Bishops, and twenty-nine deputies spoke against.[10] After five minutes of silent prayer, the vote was taken, the resolution was passed—and then deputies opposed to the change read a statement of dissent into the record. We'd come a long way, but there was no forgetting that we still had a long way to go.

No Turning Back

In 1994, House of Deputies President Pamela Chinnis sat on a General Convention panel on sexism and recalled participating in a similar event at the 1976 convention when she was presiding officer of the Triennial Meeting of the Women of the Church:

> Then we believed that dismantling the legal barriers that kept women out of the governance and ordained ministry

---

8   Richard Norris, Eugene R. Fairweather, J. E. Griffiss, Albert T. Mollegen, "Report on the Validity of the Philadelphia Ordinations," Diocese of Rochester, 15, as quoted in Darling, *New Wine*, 226.

9   Mark Kurlansky, *1968: The Year That Rocked the World* (New York: Random House, 2004), 311–12.

10 Pamela Darling, "25 Years Ago: The Struggle to Authorize Women's Ordination," http://arc.episcopalchurch.org/women/two/25yearsagao.htm (accessed December 4, 2013).

of the Church would eliminate inequity and prejudice, and today we can mark significant progress toward that goal. But when I looked back at my notes for that 1976 panel I was struck by how much remains unfulfilled. I said then,

As women seek liberation from the restrictions which have lim-ited them to a very narrow range of roles and activities, tension develops—because the basic framework of society is still essen-tially a male-oriented and dominated one. While it is less so now than in the past, the traditional male-oriented societal pat-terns, customs and thought-forms are still dominant. Sexism runs very deep in our history and culture.[11]

That watershed 1976 General Convention was my only experience of General Convention without the leadership of women. I was first elected deputy from the Diocese of Ohio in 1991, and except for one triennium (2000–2003, when we were ably led by President George Werner and Vice President Vince Currie), either the presi-dent or vice president of the House has been a woman. But in 1997, I had direct experience of Pam Chinnis's warning that sexism still ran deep.

In April of that year, I attended a meeting hastily convened by Presiding Bishop Edmond Browning to forestall a crisis at the upcoming General Convention. Although ordaining women had been canonically required for nearly twenty-one years, some bishops—a number of whom later broke away from The Episcopal Church—insisted that the canon adopted in 1976 (Canon III.8.1) was permissive rather than mandatory and continued to reject ordained ministry by women. In a lengthy presentation to the group, I set forth the canonical and political necessity for the Convention to clarify that the relevant canon be implemented as imperative.

I also reminded the meeting that the "Statement of Conscience" adopted by the all-male House of Bishops in 1977 and often cited as reason not to permit women's ordained ministry had never been affirmed by General Convention and was therefore not binding

---

11 Pamela Chinnis. *Decently and In Order: On Being the Church as the Century Turns, Selected Reflections of Pamela P. Chinnis* (Cincinnati: Forward Movement, 2000), 137–38, emphasis in original.

on the church. My written presentation, greatly enhanced by the Reverend Carol Cole Flanagan's powerful imagery, reads:

> Those bishops opposed to the ordination of women may use conscience as a shield, but they really must not, in conscience, use conscience as a sword. They may be shielded from having to ordain a woman, but they may not institutionalize their consciences in an entire diocese by preventing women from testing their vocation, by refusing to license them, or by preventing parishes from calling them solely on account of their sex.

We prevailed in 1997, but in 2000, when three dioceses—San Joaquin, Fort Worth, and Quincy—still refused to accept women as priests, General Convention passed Resolution A045[12] creating a task force to "visit, interview, assess and assist" those dioceses with an action plan to comply with the canons. Eight years later, those dioceses, still refusing to ordain women, had left The Episcopal Church. Sexism does, indeed, run very deep.

Drawing a Bigger Circle

Although the House of Deputies had sometimes lagged behind the House of Bishops in recognizing women's authority and equality, once women were admitted, the deputies began to lead the church on some of the essential social justice issues of the last several decades. As women, people of color, and lesbian, gay, bisexual, and transgender (LGBT) Christians have taken their rightful places in the House of Deputies and the wider church, the circle of leadership has been drawn wider and the church has been changed.

But, as Pam Chinnis pointed out twenty years ago, much of the promise of female leadership in The Episcopal Church remains unfulfilled. While women have ascended to the highest levels of authority in the General Convention, search committees at large endowed congregations and diocesan conventions are still reluctant to elect women as rectors and diocesan bishops. We are in danger of losing women's leadership in the House of Bishops within the next decade

---

12 General Convention, *Journal of the General Convention of . . . The Episcopal Church, Denver, 2000* (New York: General Convention, 2001), 340.

unless we can break through this glass ceiling still being imposed not by canonical restrictions but by decision makers at the grass roots.

We've also learned in the last several decades that progress is not always linear and that it is too easy to pit ourselves against each other. In 2006, several days after the historic election of Katharine Jefferts Schori as The Episcopal Church's first female presiding bishop, the House of Deputies succumbed to pressure from bishops to pass resolution B033, which imposed a *de facto* moratorium on the consecration of LGBT people to the episcopate. Faced with what ultimately proved to be a false choice, deputies agreed to sidetrack equality for LGBT people in order to provide their new female presiding bishop with leverage at otherwise all-male meetings of Anglican Communion primates and to ensure that our church's bishops would be invited to the 2008 Lambeth Conference. The "B" on Resolution B033[13] denotes that it was submitted by bishops; it is notable that the 2009 resolution that put us back on the track toward LGBT equality in the church was named D025[14] because it was submitted by Deputy Rebecca Snow, a laywoman, and endorsed by Deputies Thomas A. Little, a layman, and Ruth A. Meyers, a clergy woman. I chaired the House of Deputies legislative Committee on World Mission to which the legislation was referred.

We are currently at risk for a different kind of backsliding. While in 2012 forty-eight percent of deputies were women, only eleven percent were women of color. Of those women, four were Latina, three were Asian women, six were indigenous, and thirty-four were black or African-American. The average age of the black female deputies in 2012 was sixty-five, and the youngest of those deputies was forty-nine. Without identifying and mentoring younger leaders, we are in danger of losing the gifts, perspectives, and voices of black female deputies within the next decade.

Our continuing quest to make the church more like the kingdom of God in its diversity and unity is also being put to the test by the need to restructure for twenty-first-century ministry. Reducing the involvement of clergy and lay leaders, many of whom are women, in the name of restructuring might be a quick budget fix, but it could

---

13 General Convention, *Journal of the General Convention of . . . The Episcopal Church, Columbus, 2006* (New York: General Convention, 2007), 650–53.

14 General Convention, *Journal of the General Convention of . . . The Episcopal Church, Anaheim, 2009* (New York: General Convention, 2009), 627–28.

have devastating consequences for the church if it reduces the leadership of women, LGBT people, and people of color.

The risk exists in the House of Bishops, too: today most women bishops serve as suffragans or are retired, and some restructuring proposals seek to reduce or eliminate the ability of bishops in these circumstances to vote and speak in their house. Bishop Catharine Roskam said in the House of Bishops' debate about a well-intentioned 2012 proposal to make presiding bishop a half-time position that it seemed to her unlikely that such a proposal would have been put forward if the incumbent were a man. Although it is essential that any restructuring measures define and clarify the executive power held by the corporate structure of the church, we must fight against the often unconscious urge to devalue leadership positions simply because they are currently held by women.

Although we must be vigilant about maintaining the leadership of women and people of color as restructuring unfolds, we must also recognize that one unfortunate legacy of the long, hard struggle to eliminate canonical discrimination against women and LGBT people is that too much of our energy and vigilance has been required to secure and maintain rights within the church. And that has meant that too much of our work for equality in the last forty years has disproportionately benefited women in the church who are white, privileged, and educated.

As I wrote in a 2013 essay about gender violence for The Episcopal Church's Global Partnerships blog, if we Episcopalians can mount the kind of effort to end gender-based violence and the war on poor women and children that manifests itself in food stamp cuts and challenges to reproductive health care that we mounted to achieve the ordination of women, I am confident we can get results. I am also confident that the House of Deputies will lead the way.

GAY CLARK JENNINGS is president of the House of Deputies and is the first ordained woman to hold that post. She was ordained to the priesthood in 1979 and has served as a hospital chaplain, a parish priest, canon to the ordinary in the Diocese of Ohio, and associate director of CREDO, a church wellness program. Jennings has chaired the General Convention legislative committees on Structure, World Mission, Communications, and Canons and was a member of the Presiding

Bishop's Special Committee on Dialogue on Women in the Episcopate formed in 1986 by Presiding Bishop Browning, and the Committee for Dialogue on Canon III.8.1 established by the 1994 General Convention. Jennings is The Episcopal Church's clergy representative to the Anglican Consultative Council and a founding steering committee member of the Chicago Consultation, which supports the full inclusion of gay, lesbian, bisexual, and transgender Christians. She is a graduate of Colgate University and Episcopal Divinity School.

CHAPTER 9

Women and the Episcopate: Looking Back and Looking Forward

Catherine S. Roskam

On June 10, 1995, I was elected bishop suffragan of the Diocese of New York, and consecrated January 27, 1996, the fourth woman in The Episcopal Church and the fifth in the Anglican Communion to be ordained bishop. No protests or demonstrations marred the solemnities of the day, as they had the consecrations of the women before me, nor did any for the women consecrated after me. It seemed as if the church had turned a corner. The blossoming support for women's ordination to all orders was met with the resentful acquiescence of the opposition and their reluctant acknowledgement that, protests notwithstanding, the church was moving in the direction of the full inclusion of women.

I loved my sixteen years serving as a bishop in New York. It was to that particular episcopacy I felt most deeply called. It did not take long before I was no longer "the female bishop," but simply one of the bishops of New York who happened to be a woman. That acceptance strengthened and nourished me for the work in The Episcopal Church and the Anglican Communion, where the "female" qualifier lasted a good deal longer.

There is a schizoid element to being a bishop, a dual responsibility to Diocese (episcopacy) and House of Bishops (historic episcopate) that is sometimes complementary in nature and sometimes held in tension. Episcopal searches are generally geared to a particular episcopacy. I am embarrassed to say, I never gave much thought to the episcopate, *per se*, until I attended my first House of Bishops meeting in March of 1996.

My first surprise was the matter of time. Within the Diocese of New York, I was expected, quite reasonably I thought, to spend eighty percent of my time in the region to which I was then assigned and the remaining twenty percent split between the other two areas. At my first House of Bishops meeting I learned I would also be expected to attend two bishops' meetings a year and participate on a committee which met three times a year. Something was wrong with the original 100 percent equation, for here were responsibilities that would demand yet another third of my time, if one included travel, preparation, and follow-up. The cumulative two months a year away from family and diocese in the middle of visitation season and the school year was a stress factor in and of itself.

But it was not simply the tug of war over the demands of time. As a woman and as a New Yorker, those two contexts were like different planets. The Diocese of New York is a very diverse place, with women and men of all ages, people of color, and many different ethnicities integrated into the diocesan system at every level. The House of Bishops was and still is comprised overwhelmingly of older white men. As a woman in New York I was fully integrated into the system. In the House of Bishops I had minority status.

Writing about the House of Bishops is challenging for me. I see before me the faces of dear friends and colleagues who loved their dioceses as I loved mine, who poured themselves out in service to the people of God.

Many were committed to working for justice and peace and the dignity of every human being,[1] and the full inclusion of women. Many were indispensable allies in the struggle for women's ordination and most were intentionally welcoming to us in the House. I see them as fellow laborers in the field, even those with whom I differed on social issues.

And yet despite this, I found participation in the House of Bishops costly, both psychologically and spiritually. Despite the best

---

1 Paraphrase of a part of the baptismal covenant in the Book of Common Prayer, 305: "Will you strive for justice and peace among all people, and respect the dignity of every human being?"

intentions and overt welcoming of male bishops, I often felt like a stranger in a strange land.

I am not going to spend time on those who were overtly opposed to women's ordination. Dealing with them, or more accurately, being ignored by them, was unpleasant, but not puzzling. What needs some parsing is why those who meant well still created an atmosphere in which I as a woman did not feel at home.

First it must be said that in commenting on the House of Bishops, one must bear in mind that it is a concept and not an existential reality. Only a variety of Houses of Bishops exist, each meeting shifting and changing its membership, its purpose, its agenda, and with every triennial, a portion of its leadership as well. I don't think I ever attended a meeting at which no impending retirement was announced or no new bishop welcomed.

In addition to changing membership, a new presiding bishop is elected every nine years currently (formerly every twelve), each one helping to shape the character and movement of the current house as a conductor shapes the expression of a symphony.

People who are not bishops rarely take into consideration the fluid nature of the House. Instead, they tend to characterize the House of Bishops according to some action or inaction in which they are most interested. Bishops are not guiltless in this either. For most of my first decade as a bishop, I experienced the House, still reeling and reacting to the rancor and the personalities of the General Convention in Phoenix in 1991, attempting to heal itself. A great deal of time and energy was spent on it over the years. I am not sure how much we actually healed those wounds or whether they became increasingly irrelevant to a newer and often younger house whose members had no part in that experience and whose opinions in support of women's ordination and gay ordination were beginning to coalesce into a significant majority, furthered by the defection of some, but not all, who disagreed.

But in an ever flowing stream, continuity may suffer. The progress one makes in any triennium or during any primate's term may slip away in the next.

Elements That Have Worked in Women's Favor

Over the years, some changes made in the way the House conducts itself have helped to facilitate the incorporation of women, although they were not instituted for that purpose. Progress has been made in other ways as well.

1. The use of round tables, begun a few years before I became a bishop, fostered a more egalitarian relational model, rather than the former linear seating by seniority. The tables allow for more personal sharing, giving bishops the opportunity to form deeper relationship with each other. It becomes more difficult to demonize, objectify, characterize, or stereotype one another. It's worth noting that for years before the ultimate defection of the dissident bishops, most refused to participate in these gatherings and processes, quarantining themselves in a sense, lest they be "infected" by the often mind-changing experience of getting to know one's opponent as a human being and true lover of Christ.

2. True acceptance and respect for the ordination of women developed over time. Although the majority of bishops made a point of welcoming women bishops in the early years, a minority made it clear that they considered us laywomen. No one currently in the House to my knowledge disputes the fact that the women in the House really are bishops.

3. A good many of the male bishops are, in my opinion, truly feminist, i.e., they believe that women are fully human, with equal right to autonomy, authority, and agency as men.

4. I can attest to the formation of deep friendships among bishops, without respect to gender.

5. The establishment of CREDO for Bishops served to further break down barriers among bishops.

6. Indaba, introduced at Lambeth 2008, became an effective tool for communicating in depth. The continued use of Indaba has enabled bishops to explore fully the questions before us before they come to a vote on the floor of the House.

7. In 2006 we elected a woman as presiding bishop.

At the Heart of It

Despite the progress made so far and despite differing personalities, changing hot-button issues, and other vicissitudes of time, it is true and obvious that the House of Bishops remains predominantly older, white, and male.[2] While the median age has begun to drop somewhat over the last decade, the other two aspects of the house—race and gender—have remained constant.

Addressing racial issues is not in the purview of this article. But the fact that the racial proportions of the population are not reflected in The Episcopal Church at large pushes the problem of discrimination at least in part to the realm of evangelism and welcome into congregations themselves.

What is different in considering women's place in the House of Bishops is that we are not a minority in the church. We are more than half of church participants, both in The Episcopal Church and in the Anglican Communion. While women make up at least a significant proportion of the House of Deputies, the membership of women in the House of Bishops continues to hover around five percent.

At the time of General Convention in 2000, there were eight women bishops. A journalist began a question by saying, "Now that women bishops are on the ascendancy in the House . . ." Gay Jennings, one of the briefers from the House of Deputies, and currently its president, quickly interposed. "Eight women in a house of 150 to 200 active bishops does not constitute an ascendancy!" In my active years our numbers rose to thirteen active women bishops at one point, but when I retired, that number had fallen back into single digits. Ordained women in TEC make up more than forty percent of clergy[3] and yet the number of active women bishops can't seem to break a baker's dozen.

Why is this so? And how can we address this challenge moving forward?

Status Quo Dynamics

1. The House of Bishops is a system, and systems perpetuate themselves if they are not examined and consciously changed.

    Like the congregation that mysteriously does not grow past eighty-five percent of its seating capacity, homogeneous

---

2 I intentionally omit the matter of sexual preference, as that characteristic is not readily observable and a much more complex issue. Suffice it to say that gay and lesbian members of the house will most likely resonate with the observations and issues raised with regard to women's participation in the House.

3 "Called to Serve," publication of the Church Pension Group.

systems tend to resist the introduction of difference even if individuals within the system would welcome it. Rheinhold Niebuhr explores this dilemma philosophically in his great classic, *Moral Man and Immoral Society*. Sociologist Thomas Schelling articulates the problem in a more pragmatic way in "Dynamic Models of Segregation" in which he states, "There is no simple correspondence of individual incentive to collective results."[4] As Schelling points out, in a binary system, neither group makes choices that lead to their own minority.

2. The House of Bishops is still a male system.

One has only to compare gender-dominant groups such as fraternities to sororities or men's groups to women's groups to know that all-male systems differ from all-female systems. In order to integrate men and women into one system, we have to be able to compare gender dominant systems without judgment. One is not better than the other. They are simply different.

For millennia in Christianity and for over two centuries in the American succession, the House of Bishops was completely male. The composition of the House now is ninety-five percent male, so the expectation that a bishop is male at any meeting of the House is still going to be met more than nine times out of ten. Women bishops remain atypical. The expectation of maleness remains the backdrop to the scene.

A gathering of women in as small a number as three often suggests threat to that expectation. At the very least such a gathering of women draws attention. How often have I and my sisters sitting together heard "jokes" or comments about how we are "plotting" or "planning a takeover." Why would that even come to mind if men weren't invested, however unconsciously, in preserving the privilege majority provides? Why is it that women sitting together draw comment while no one remarks at the many tables of men only? I finally learned to deal with this by saying with a smile, "Yes, we are. And you had better be shaking in your boots." It always seemed to relieve the tension. And I certainly felt better.

---

4 Thomas C. Schelling, "Dynamic Models of Segregation" *Journal of Mathematical Sociology* 1 (1971): 143ff.

The numerical dominance of men in the episcopate may be at least one reason some qualified women priests refuse nomination to episcopal searches, thereby helping to perpetuate the maleness of the system themselves.

3.   The "marking "of women is significant.

When maleness is normative in a particular context, women are what Deborah Tannen calls "marked." She begins with linguistics:

> The unmarked form of a word carries the meaning that goes without saying, what you think of when you're not thinking anything special. . . . The unmarked forms of most English words also convey "male." Being male is the unmarked case. We have endings, such as *ess* and *ette*, to mark words as female. Unfortunately, marking words for female also, by association, tends to mark them for frivolousness. Would you feel safe entrusting your life to a doctorette?[5]

Dr. Tannen continues with the discussion of the marked character of women's clothing in the workplace—there is no analogy for women to the widely accepted workplace uniformity of slacks, blazer, loafers, or oxfords and the unremarkable tie—and I would add in the context of ordained women in the church, no analogy to the uniformity of the dark suit, clergy shirt, and collar. Women clergy who adopt "the uniform" in dark pantsuit, clergy shirt, and collar are nevertheless "marked" by this understandable practice of ecclesial cross-dressing. Clergy "blouses" have emerged in the Whipple and Almy catalogues, and the wearing of any one of them is "marked," the color and cut noticed and interpreted. Even the most feminine of clergy blouses is usually still worn with the male collar.

Language and apparel are not minor matters. They are metaphors for a worldview held, often unconsciously, by people in certain contexts, that no matter how qualified a woman is, maleness is normative.

---

5 Deborah Tannen, *Talking from 9 to 5: Women and Men at Work* (New York: Harper Collins Publishers), 109–10.

When working outside the "female realm" of home and family, there is still almost nothing about us that "goes without saying," even today. Ministering in a diocese that more often than not addressed male priests as Father, I struggled throughout my priesthood with the question, "What shall we call you?" At last, I thought when I became a bishop, I won't have to deal with THAT question anymore, since "bishop" is not gender specific. Wrong. I was still asked the question. In return I asked the person how he or she addressed our male bishops. Usually it was Bishop (Last Name). I would then ask to be addressed in the same manner. It was like walking someone through a very simple math problem whose answer still left many obviously perplexed. They were not expecting to address a woman as bishop, even though they supported my consecration as such.

4. There are differences in communication and management styles.

Nowhere is this basic and largely unconscious assumption of male normativeness more destructive to women's advancement than in the areas of communication and management styles. For women, these are "damned if you do, damned if you don't" areas. As Tannen points out:

> There is a mountain of research attesting that when females and males get together in groups, the females are more likely to change their styles to adapt to the presence of males—whether they are adults or children.[6]

Perhaps the most heartbreaking examples of the latter can be found in Mary Pipher's wake-up call of a book, *Reviving Ophelia: Saving the Selves of Adolescent Girls*, which reveals the extent to which girls sacrifice their sense of self in deference to society's pressures and expectations of gender roles, as early as eleven years of age.[7]

These pressures and expectations never disappear as a woman matures and enters into the workplace. They just

---

6 Tannen, *Talking from 9 to 5,* 119.
7 Mary Pipher, *Reviving Ophelia: Saving the Selves of Adolescent Girls* (New York: Riverhead Books, 1994).

go underground, affecting women and men, often unconsciously and always systemically.

Communication style is closely linked to management style. In my experience, women's communication and management styles are more closely allied with the communication and management styles of other cultures than they are with American workplace values. Women in the workplace often soften communication as a means of encouragement and promoting the work of the group. A woman will often use "we" instead of "I" when it comes to successes, even if she is the sole reason for the success. Women often help colleagues and subordinates "save face." It is not our style to put ourselves forward. This is even truer in a Christian context, where self-denial and self-effacement are taught and rewarded—in women, but not so much in men. Scriptural texts of submission are still used in some contexts to suppress the independence, authority, and agency of women. To its shame, The Episcopal Church took half a century more than secular culture to arrive at women's suffrage. We do not escape our history that quickly or that completely.

In any case, gentleness and self-effacement in communication and management styles are often erroneously interpreted as incompetence, weakness, or lack of leadership ability. Episcopal searches do not take these differences into consideration.

Women who choose a more masculine style of leadership will be dubbed "strident," "abrasive," "aggressive." The first two words are rarely used to describe men, while the third is often used as a compliment.

5. Primal factors are also important.

Perhaps the great obstacle to women's entry into the episcopate is the unconscious resistance, not to women's ordination *per se*, but to the authority of women. It is, at least in part, behind the question, "What shall we call you?" Tannen posits that men especially have the propensity to experience women in authority as Mother. She cites many examples from her research, and anecdotally I could cite quite a few from my own experience.

The psychological development of boys needs to be different from the psychological development of girls with regard to separation from the mother and developing gender identity. Since Freud's positing of "The Oedipus Complex," psychologists have not been in agreement about the method of differentiation, but most agree it exists, expressed in various theories of separation or attachment that have continued to evolve even up to the present. Tannen suggests that our [women and men alike] primary images of female authority come from motherhood.[8] I would like to suggest that this is especially true for older men, who may have had less opportunity to have experienced women as classmates, colleagues, and superiors in their lifetime.

Some Suggestions for the Way Forward

1. Examine sexism and systemic resistance to change.

    We have a black president, racism is not gone, and the conversation continues. We have a female presiding bishop, sexism is not gone, but the conversation has not even begun. The House of Bishops missed that discussion the first time around in the 60s and early 70s because women were not in their midst. And even in the 80s, Pam Darling's indispensible book, *New Wine: The Story of Women Transforming Leadership and Power in the Episcopal Church,*[9] reminds us "that [The Rt. Rev. Barbara] Harris's only access to the drafting process of statement related to women in the episcopate was via the small group reporting process." Darling goes on to say that this "suggests that an old pattern was still in place, rendering women virtually invisible and men incapable of hearing their voices. . . . It was certainly not the first time men had debated issues directly affecting women without inviting their participation, nor would it be the last."

    At General Convention in 2012, when asked if she thought a presiding bishop could do an effective job while also being the bishop of a diocese, Katharine Jefferts Schori articulated

---

8 Tannen, *Talking from 9 to 5,* 161; and all of chapter Six, "She's the Boss: Women and Authority," 160–203, has immensely valuable points to make on this subject.

9 Pamela W. Darling, *New Wine: The Story of Women Transforming Leadership and Power in the Episcopal Church* (Cambridge, MA: Cowley Publications, 1994), 186ff.

quite clearly that she did not think so. Nevertheless, the discussion continued as if she had not spoken, a discussion I firmly believe would not have happened had the presiding bishop been a man.

While antiracism training and listening to gay men and lesbians have been incorporated into House of Bishops programming, no training for gender sensitivity or antigender discrimination has to my knowledge taken place.[10] The time has come.

2. Become more familiar with the literature.

"Called to Serve: A Study of Clergy Careers, Clergy Wellness, and Clergy Women" was prepared by the Church Pension Fund, in cooperation with CREDO and the (now sadly and inappropriately defunct) Episcopal Church Center's Office of Women's Ministry, in response to resolutions of the 75th General Convention in 2006. It demystifies and documents the complex factors that result in the discrimination women clergy experience.

Although this document was presented to the House of Bishops, there was no significant follow-up by that body to my knowledge. Yet the facts in this study are pure gold for any bishop or church body who truly wishes to effect change in the area of women and the episcopate. The more that valued women clergy are in the church at large, the more they will be valued and taken seriously as candidates in episcopal searches.

New Wine, cited above, is the most comprehensive history I have found of women in The Episcopal Church. Deborah Tannen's writing, particularly about men and women in the workplace, is immensely helpful in an objective and illuminating way. Thomas Schelling and other sociologists writing in the 70s about segregation are worth reading, not only for antiracism, but by extrapolation for antisexism. If we consider gender-based shared experience as a form of culture, Eric Law's *The Wolf Shall Dwell with the Lamb* can be of

---

10 The one exception was the stellar presentation organized by Jane Williams and the bishops' spouses at Lambeth 2008 concerning violence against women.

assistance.[11] Much more is available for those who are interested in pursuing this topic. (If we had an Office of Women's Ministries we might have had a bibliography ready to hand!)

3. Give attention to episcopal searches.

    Some bishops have said we should simply "trust the Holy Spirit" when it comes to women and episcopal searches. About what other justice issue might we say that? And how does the Holy Spirit work, if not through people? Some dioceses have more success in recruiting women candidates than others. We could learn from one another.

    Let me be clear. This is not about electing women no matter what their qualifications. This is about evening out the playing field for qualified women, so that their candidacies are not scuttled by the old expectation, still true in ninety-five percent of cases, as elaborated earlier in this essay, that bishops are (should be) male.

4. Embrace the authority of the office we hold.

    We as ordained women need to claim and embrace the authority vested in us by the church by virtue of the office we hold either as priest or bishop, even if we exercise that authority differently from men. Hierarchy is not a dirty word. Hierarchy can be exercised with grace and humility.[12] Women entering the system have a unique opportunity to lead us in that direction. We are still The Episcopal Church, not The Episcopal-ish Church.

What Happens When We Are Successful . . .

Retirement has enabled me to reflect more deeply on the vocation of bishop, but while my time in the Diocese of New York has been brought to its bittersweet conclusion, I find my time in the House of Bishops still unresolved. A great deal happened in the church and in the episcopate with regard to the acceptance of women in the sixteen years I served actively in the House, yet some things remain painfully the same in the church and the world.

---

11 Eric H. F. Law, *The Wolf Shall Dwell with the Lamb* (St. Louis, MO: Chalice Press, 1993).

12 Tannen, *Talking from 9 to 5*, 213ff.

Once women and minorities enter a respected and well-paid field of endeavor, salaries go down, and power begins to reside elsewhere. For instance, once women and minorities entered the field of medicine as doctors instead of nurses and aides, power and wealth shifted to insurance companies and hospital administrations run primarily by white males.

What will happen when women bishops really are in ascendancy—when our numbers begin to reach twenty, thirty, or forty percent? My guess is that the office of bishop will have less authority and lower remuneration. Whether or not that will be good for the church and the people of God is another discussion. What's interesting is that those considerations almost always arise when women and minorities begin entering a better-paid and prestigious field in numbers greater than twenty percent.

Going forward, will the church be able to model a different, more equitable outcome? Dare we hope for a House of Bishops where majority easily shifts back and forth between women and men in an atmosphere of mutual respect and gratitude for complementarity? It's a kingdom vision, I know, but with God, anything is possible.

In addition to her pastoral ministries as a bishop, **CATHERINE ROSKAM** was involved in mission both global and local. She is the founder of the Global Women's Fund of the Diocese of New York dedicated to educating Anglican women in the developing world; All Our Children, an initiative in support of public education in the US; and cofounder of The Carpenter's Kids, a partnership with the Diocese of Central Tanganyika which now enables over 7,000 AIDS orphans in Tanzania to go to school. Roskam was a member of the Anglican Consultative Council for nine years, on the Executive Council of the Episcopal Church for six, and also on the House of Bishops Theology Committee. She is a graduate of General Seminary and an associate of the Society of St. John the Evangelist. Catherine and her husband, Philip, now live in California where they delight in playing with their four-year-old grandson.

CHAPTER 10

From Women Priests to Feminist Ecclesiology?

Stephen Burns

"Suppose," Ann Loades, an esteemed British feminist theologian, asked, "we were to try and shift a marginal element in the Christian tradition into the mainstream in spirituality *and* in doctrine, what effects might it have? What could we expect it to do for us?"[1] In what follows, I wonder about these questions with respect to women in the ordained presbyterate. The recognition of the leadership of women that was signaled by the ordination of women in The Episcopal Church was certainly a shift to bring something marginal within— though not absent from—the Christian tradition into its mainstream, at least in one small corner of the world. What effects did it have? How did it change us?

Of course, much may depend on what contours and boundaries are assumed to define the "us" in the latter question. Who's us? First, the "us" is "feminists," and I follow Loades's own view that not all women should be assumed to be feminists just as neither should it be assumed that all feminists are women. I write as one unambiguously committed to women as priests, or more to the point, to all forms of ministry being equally accessible to differently gendered persons.

---

1 Ann Loades, *Searching for Lost Coins: Explorations in Christianity and Feminism* (London: SPCK, 1987), 96ff, from which I quote in this opening section and subsequently.

But, then, the "us" is much, much wider, and within a wider view the effects on the presbyterate itself certainly need to keep in mind the *shared ministry* of women and men in that particular form of holy orders.

In any case, Loades sagely warns of not "claiming too much" for whatever shifts may be possible from margins to mainstream (or might we say "malestream" or "manstream"). She takes as a vivid, grisly example the remark of philosopher Anthony Flew: "Someone tells us that God loves us as a father loves his children. We are reassured. But then we see a child dying of inoperable cancer of the throat. His earthly father is driven frantic by his efforts to help, but his Heavenly Father reveals no obvious sign of concern."

Loades herself comments: "Substitute 'mother' all through, and the child will still die of inoperable cancer of the throat, just as one singer of Psalm 22 died on the cross." For Loades, language-change *might* have what she delineates as a "limited task," *if*—and emphatically if—some other conditions are met. She suggests that also in need of scrutiny are lectionaries, so we might surmise: what—and whose—stories get into them, and what—and who—is left out. She identifies liturgies as in need of scrutiny, which are of course much more than texts, but rather events constructed from layered and overlapping ceremonial scenes. Also in need of scrutiny, Loades notes, is ministry: which persons are supposed to be authorized to embody graced presence, and what they do—and don't do—once so designated. Loades very helpfully reminds us that it is crucial to remember what we might call a larger "ecology" of possibly highly problematic factors when thinking about so-called "inclusive" or "expansive" language.

When we make ministry our particular focus, the point remains that the "shift" to women priests needs to be related to a wider range of factors. Taking up Loades's trajectory of thinking, questions call into question larger contexts, demand wider attention, and require that connections are made to other foci. We should beware of claiming too much for shifts in one thing or another unless they are linked up in a wider view. On one hand, The Episcopal Church might now seem unimaginable without women in the ranks of the clergy. On the other hand, maybe not so much has changed and far too many women have "adopted as unisex"[2] styles of leadership

---

2 Gail Ramshaw, "Christian Worship from a Feminist Perspective," in *Worship Today: Understanding, Practice, Ethical Implications,* ed. Thomas F. Best and Dagmar Heller (Geneva: World Council of Churches, 2004), 209.

which, from feminist perspectives, are part of the problem. Not all women are feminists, as I have said; and neither women nor men priests may be feminist enough. In my reflections I trace some of the challenges to deeper transformation of the church through oscillations between expansive language and women's ordination, and between women's ordination and what I regard as the desperate need for prayer book revision in The Episcopal Church. I hope this illumines some broadly applicable issues as well as some very specific contradictions that need to be contested in Episcopal Church contexts.

Relating the Issues to Expansive Language

Developments in the realm of expansive language since women's ordination are themselves appropriate connections to make to questions about the effect women's ordination might be having. Such language has been diversely crafted, variously received, and sometimes rejected. Lessons of its development are instructive, not least because they impact and enact both spirituality and doctrine.

Expansive language amends inherited uses to employ more contemporary idioms for human persons. It might also seek to expand metaphors for the divine. Such shifts away from "man," "Father," "he," "Lord," "K/king," et al., were at their zenith in The Episcopal Church in *Enriching Our Worship 1*, a book determined to ditch what it called "*Paterfamilias*" depictions of God.[3] Yet there has not always been an affiliated consciousness that expanded language needs to be made congruent with a perhaps as yet largely unimagined new ceremonial style and re-visioning of space. Rosemary Radford Ruether's groundbreaking *Women-Church* is to be commended for beginning to think through the space that feminist styles of worship might invite. For examples, she refers to "conversation circles" and presents new texts for rites old and new. Also highly commendable is Letty Russell's *Church in the Round,* the title of which suggests her concern to shape space. But her proposals about round tables that decenter hierarchical leadership have remained rarely translated into physical liturgical environments and the ritual pictures deployed in them.[4] Furthermore, it

---

3 *Enriching Our Worship 1* (New York: Church Publishing, 1998), 8.

4 For further discussion of both Russell and Ruether, see Stephen Burns, "'Four in a Vestment'? Feminist Gesture for Christian Assembly," in *Presiding Like a Woman,* ed. Nicola Slee and Stephen Burns (London: SPCK, 2010), 9–19.

has far from consistently been recognized that the gender constructions which riddle inherited liturgical metaphors, and which relate to
what Gail Ramshaw characterizes as "the myth of the crown,"[5] need
to be made more humanly inclusive in a whole range of other ways.
Detrimental associations between light as goodness and darkness as
evil—which dog so much liturgy (again, not just texts, but events)—
and the implications for black and Asian persons of such associations is just one prime example of much needed change in language,
symbol, and ceremony.[6]

In the shadow of these comments, we might note that despite
recognizing that "non-verbal language—the language of gesture,
movement, sign—will always override the text of the prayer,"[7]
Enriching Our Worship 1 has amended texts, but gives no advice, nor
offers any guidance, on the wider ecology in which texts are prayed
or proclaimed. Hence, commendable for expansive language it may
be, but it is also an example of limited liturgical revision in that even
those who amend their language can remain all too vulnerable to
subverting it with ceremonial scenes which reinscribe the hierarchies
they intend their newfound language to elide.

We might also suspect that inclusive language can all-too-easily
be co-opted to the status quo by removing the language people need
to identify problems in which they are implicated. For instance, if
a community's talk is characteristically of "circles" (*a la* church in
the round) as opposed to ranks or hierarchies, we need to be certain that it reflects, rather than disguises, the social relationships in
which we are arrayed. We need to be certain that it does not in fact
obscure the categories we need to name the power dynamics, and
their ritual inscriptions, of which we may remain very much a part
if we look no further than language-change in and of itself. That
is, inclusive language can be used to mask realities: hierarchies can
be hidden by shifts in terms, and it is perhaps even possible that we
may be best to retain some exclusive language—unpalatable as it may
be for other reasons—if we are not unwittingly to hand ourselves
over to actual or potential hierarchs, despots, and megalomaniacs

---

5 Gail Ramshaw, *God Beyond Gender: Feminist Christian God Language*
   (Minneapolis, MN: Fortress Press, 1995), 59–74.
6 See Michael N. Jagessar and Stephen Burns, *Christian Worship: Postcolonial
   Perspectives* (Sheffield: Equinox, 2011), 33–50.
7 *Enriching Our Worship 1*, 16.

in our midst. Hierarchical language at least keeps us alert to their presence! Ann Loades is once more very helpful, asserting that so-called "traditional" language, for all its apparent "exclusivity," may yet powerfully "put the 'lords' of this world in their places."[8] At least sometimes. But whether or not we are convinced of this, continuing the strand in which I started: the connection needs to be made between language, space, and how power is used in it. The point also stands that inclusive language may not do for us what we might hope it will do, and it is by no means a mark or guarantor that inclusive communities have been created or safeguarded. So we need to ask about the limited task of language-change, the limited task of lectionary revision, the limited task of making more humanly inclusive ministry, and the limited task of reshaping the liturgical environment. We need then to ask how these things *conspire together* to effect change. Then it might be clearer what yet remains to be done and how limited measures may be connected to one another in order to reach toward deeper or wider effects on ecclesial contexts and the social settings of which they are a part. It is important to not naïvely believe that worship shaped by expansive language, or communities led by women priests, are somehow less vulnerable than the rest to what Johann Baptist Metz called "eulogistic evasion of what really matters."[9]

Enriching Our Worship 1 emerged in close proximity to other denominations' best efforts with expansive language,[10] and in many places and many traditions the 1990s saw the genre flourish. Twenty years later expansive language advocates and supporters of women's ministry are more sanguine, for reasons just now beginning to surface: language can all-too-easily be put to reality-disguising mischief. We are learning to recognize the reality that women adopting certain inherited styles of ministry don't do much to change things for the better. Inclusive language may inoculate against more comprehensive change—and so may the ordination of women, if what

---

8 Ann Loades, "Finding New Sense in the Sacramental," in *The Gestures of God: Explorations in Sacramentality,* ed. Geoffrey Rowell and Christine Hall (London: Continuum, 2004), 71.

9 Karl Rahner and Johann Baptist Metz, *The Courage to Pray* (New York: Crossroad, 1981), 20.

10 For example, the United Church of Christ's *New Century Hymnal* (Cleveland, OH: Pilgrim Press, 1995) and the Roman Catholic Church's never-authorized *Psalter* (Chicago, IL: Liturgy Training Publications, 1995).

we hope for is an end to patriarchy. Change for the better should not be the burden of women alone: the differently gendered *together* need to reimagine the role of ordained ministry. These recognitions sharpen the question of what is involved in a feminist ecclesiology (theology of church) which seeks profounder transformation of Christian assembly, its patterns of leadership, and its images of the divine.

Feminist Ecclesiology

It is becoming clearer that it is one thing to change language and quite another to enable affective change through deeply internalized alternative imagery which differs from the traditional cluster around the *Paterfamilias*. Juliana Claassens's *Mourner, Mother, Midwife* is an attractive recent rehabilitation of marginal Old Testament imagery for the divine, and she is hopeful that "gradually these female metaphors work in the minds and hearts of listeners to bring awareness of the relational aspects of God."[11] Yet another excellent recent work, Jennie S. Knight's *Feminist Mysticism and Images of God*,[12] is a sobering exploration of such hope, indicating just how long such gradual awareness may take, even for those most committed to it. At the same time, some recent moves in expansive language have shifted focus from God to Christ, attempting, for instance, to reimagine Christ as "Christa." This, for all its verve, is not likely to provide any "short-cuts" to transformed understandings, let alone transformed communities. Even so, Nicola Slee's poem "At the table of Christa" is a powerful depiction of what might well be regarded as key marks of a feminist ecclesiology. It presents in poetic mode convictions spelled out in prose by the likes of Ruether and Russell, as well as in Slee's own distillation of feminist ecclesiology in her primer *Faith and Feminism*.[13] However one responds to Christa, the poem depicts a community worth being a part of:

---

11 L. Juliana M. Claassens, *Mourner, Mother, Midwife: Reimagining God's Delivering Presence in the Old Testament* (Louisville, KY: Westminster John Knox Press, 2012), 96.

12 Jennie S. Knight, *Feminist Mysticism and Images of God: A Practical Theology* (St. Louis, MO: Chalice Press, 2011).

13 Nicola Slee, *Faith and Feminism: An Introduction to Christian Feminist Theology* (London: DLT, 2004), 83–94.

At the table of Christa
There is no seat of honour
for all are honoured
There is no etiquette
except the performance of grace
There is no dress code
except the garments of honesty
There is no fine cuisine
other than the bread of justice[14]

To thicken imagination of what this might mean in practice, Janet Walton's concentrated cluster of proposals for "feminist liturgy" can constructively be read alongside Slee's poem. Walton suggests, "Horizontal gestures prevail in feminist liturgies," and they depict "equality and interdependence; they affirm God known among us." Further:

Generally we do not look up to find God. . . . We pray with our eyes open and without bowing our heads. . . . Bowing our heads for a blessing, as Marjorie Procter-Smith points out, is "a non-reciprocal action." . . . Closing one's eyes is dangerous in an unjust society. . . . Feminist liturgies intend to provide occasions to practice gestures of resistance and expressions of shared power.[15]

These writers give some concrete clues as to what kinds of liturgical gestures might need to be enlarged alongside expansive language, as we also reconsider what space such words and gestures require.

Such liturgical visions can themselves be brought to wider proposals about feminist ecclesiology, such as have been elaborated by Natalie Watson.[16] Watson rightly insists that "the question of women's ordination needs to be discussed in a wider context of what it means to be church."[17] She points out that some traditions of women-

---

14 Nicola Slee, *Seeking the Risen Christa* (London: SPCK, 2011), 56.
15 Janet Walton, *Feminist Liturgy: A Matter of Justice* (Collegeville, MN: Liturgical Press, 2000), 36–37.
16 Natalie Watson, *Introducing Feminist Ecclesiology* (Sheffield: Sheffield Academic Press, 2002).
17 Watson, *Feminist Ecclesiology*, 77. In this section I quote liberally from Watson's chapter on ministry.

church have rejected any idea of ordained leadership, in favor of "structures that enable ministries of mutual empowerment," however such structures are then imagined. Others within the women-church movement have, she narrates, taken a more pragmatic approach and regarded it as essential to engage with inherited structures. These latter seek "transformation from within," looking to infiltrate the centers of power in their institutions, with the intent that they will "enter hierarchical structures in order to subvert them and break them down." For her own part, Watson suggests that feminists "have to recognize the subversive potential of entering the ordained ministry and of being able to lead a church of women and men into being part of the new liberated humanity." Is this, though, what we have seen? It is all-too-obvious to ask if, on the basis of the last forty years, it is expecting too much.

To help us make that judgment, Watson gives numerous further clues to what a feminist ecclesiology might look like when manifest in practices, not so much liturgically focused, like Walton, but more in terms of ministerial style. For example:

> A feminist reconception of ecclesiology which retains a concept of ordained ministry as a possibility has to emphasize the importance of a functional approach to understanding the significance of that specific ministry.[18]

Feminist ecclesiology, she avers, is concerned with radical equality and democracy, which means that all are called—indeed, ordained—by virtue of their baptism. This conviction, in The Episcopal Church, might well be taken to cohere with the "baptismal ecclesiology" that is sometimes, perhaps rather optimistically, said to be characteristic of the current Episcopal edition of the Book of Common Prayer. In other ecclesial traditions, similar conviction is conveyed by the vesting of newly baptized persons in a "baptismal stole"[19]—a daring appropriation of a traditional symbol of ordination to the prior and broader context of baptism. With or without such symbolic mediation, feminist ecclesiology is likely to insist that within a community of baptismal ministry the need for leadership may be pragmatic, or

---

18 Watson, *Feminist Ecclesiology*, 75.
19 United Church of Canada, *Celebrate God's Presence: A Book of Services* (Toronto, ON: United Church Press, 2000), 354.

functional, but that it does not involve any change in status of one designated to lead the community. As Watson articulates her convictions, in feminist ecclesiology leadership is shared; it celebrates difference, and must be seen to seek justice; authority involves "no distinction between ranks or peoples of different status." Further, such authority is grounded in clear manifestation that "any ministry of proclaiming the gospel in a particular community is rooted in listening, in hearing into speech," with "shared authority enabl[ing] all members of a community to break cycles of oppression and secrecy."

While Loades cautions that not too much should be expected of one disconnected, isolated, "inclusive" shift or another, Watson contends that "it is important not to see shared authority as an ideal." Rather we should relate it to the realities of having to listen to unpopular opinions, transparency in financial matters, anyone being able to "name the agenda," commitment to "hidden agendas" being brought out into the open, constructive approaches to conflict, and refusal to "sweep difficult situations under the carpet." These are all demanding marks of her feminist perspective on church.

The shared authority of which Watson speaks might wisely be regarded as a spiritual discipline. She is clear that it is also embedded in Christian doctrine, relating it to an understanding echoing the image of the triune God.[20]

Episcopal Church Liturgical Revision

It may indeed be true that "for many women, seeing a woman at the altar or in the pulpit is an empowering sign of their own being church,"[21] and that this can contribute greatly to an affective sense that cognitively focused language change cannot alone achieve. In some imaginations, Eucharistic presidency involves conceiving presiders as qualified and capable to serve as a "sacrament within the sacrament."[22] At a cognitive level at least, this recognition may be taken to be as widespread of ordained women as of ordained men in The Episcopal Church. What it might involve in terms of the practice of presiders—of different genders—is more opaque, however. In an

---

20 Watson, *Feminist Ecclesiology,* 77
21 Watson, *Feminist Ecclesiology,* 73.
22 See Bruce Morrill, *Encountering Christ in the Eucharist* (Mahwah, NJ: Paulist Press, 2012), 103.

Episcopal Church context, especially problematic is the fact that the Book of Common Prayer's apparent doctrine of baptismal ecclesiology conflicts with a raft of clericalizing rubrics. William Seth Adams offers the astute diagnosis that there are "two ideas at work" in the BCP's opposite yet "entangled" theologies of ministry. Adams is clear that the two theologies of ministry in the BCP are not always "compatible," and that it is "impossible" to describe the BCP's theology of ministry "as if it were a unified theology."[23] The ensuing problems have many particular manifestations and keep coming into focus around the BCP's highly objectionable use of the term "celebrant" for the one who is only the *presiding* celebrant among *other* celebrants of the Eucharist. The presiding minister is only *one* minister amongst *all* the ministers of the church as identified in the BCP's own catechism. "Who are the ministers of the church?" receives the unambiguous answer that "the ministers of the church are laypersons, bishops, priests, and deacons."[24] As Adams notes, such a view is inconsistent and unconvincing across the book. The term "celebrant" applied to the presider hardly clarifies or proclaims that "the assembly is the celebrant of the eucharist"[25] and is from being congruent with the kind of feminist ecclesiology of which I have been inviting consideration.

In any case, the consequence of such confusion is that for practically the entire time that The Episcopal Church has welcomed women priests, the Book of Common Prayer's baptismal ecclesiology has been subverted in ceremonial scenes that inhibit the BCP's vision of baptized people. Such ceremonial scenes have themselves been constructed from the rubrics of the BCP. Especially dismal with respect to the role of the so-called "celebrant" is the BCP's cluster of rubrics relating to handling the bread and wine ("manual acts") in Eucharistic prayer. Members of the assembly are rendered passive onlookers of a ceremonial event done by clergy and a few other "assistants." This ritual action has itself become marginal in the contemporary Anglican Communion in terms of how churches have recently been revising their rites, often ditching this "Jesus tableaux" from their liturgical repertoire:

---

23 See William Seth Adams, *Moving the Furniture: Liturgical Theory, Practice, and Environment* (New York: Church Publishing, 1999), 35.

24 Book of Common Prayer, 855.

25 David R. Holeton, ed., *Our Thanks and Praise: The Eucharist in Anglicanism Today* (Toronto, ON: Anglican Book Centre, 1998), 261.

Manual acts which draw attention to the institution narrative or other portions of the [Eucharistic] prayer serve to locate consecration within a narrow portion of the text and may contradict a more contemporary understanding of eucharistic consecration.[26]

The difficulty with The Episcopal Church's practice is examined by Louis Weil who contrasts *in persona Christi* and *in persona ecclesiae* interpretations of the presider's role[27]: a "strong identification of the presider with Jesus must be questioned given our gradual recovery of a sense of the entire community being the 'celebrants' of the Eucharist." Weil argues, "A priest at the altar is not imitating Jesus at the last supper, but is presiding at an action in which the gathered people of God are full participants." Weil commends "the extraordinary theological integrity of eucharistic praise with no manual acts"[28]—the presider with arms extended in prayer (known as *orans*). Notably, Weil also reminds his readers that the *orans* position of prayer is appropriate to all celebrants, presiding or otherwise. I contend that the clerical posturing of the BCP is one of the first things that a feminist ecclesiology will need to contest. Advocates of feminist ecclesiology will also need to be alert that abandoning such rubrics and changing practices and images will need to be carefully negotiated among lay and ordained, women as well as men. It is no surprise to find Weil writing that he "had hoped at first that women might offer a fresh understanding of the presider's role, but in general they have adopted the same norm as the ordained men."[29]

It seems, then, that Loades's caution not to expect too much from one shift or another is wisely applied to The Episcopal Church's past forty years of women priests. Deeper change awaits us. I hope that in coming years, women and men together may find the courage to lead with the marks of feminist ecclesiology, and that not only will we encourage the differently gendered among the ordained presbyterate, but that we might even find the table of Christa.

---

26 Ibid., 300.
27 Weil, *Liturgical Sense*, 88–89.
28 Ibid., 100.
29 Ibid., 18.

STEPHEN BURNS is associate professor of liturgical theology and the study of Anglicanism at Episcopal Divinity School, Cambridge, Massachusetts. He is a presbyter in the Church of England who has also recently lived in Australia. His publications include *Liturgy,* SCM Studyguide (London: SCM Press, 2006); *Exchanges of Grace: Essays in Honour of Ann Loades* (coeditor with Natalie K. Watson; London: SCM Press, 2008); *Worship and Ministry: Shaped Towards God* (Melbourne: Mosaic Press, 2012); *Liturgical Spirituality* (editor; New York: Church Publishing, 2013); and *Public Theology and the Challenge of Feminism* (coeditor with Anita Monro; Sheffield: Equinox, 2014).

CHAPTER 11

May God Bless the Work of Our Hands

Winnie Varghese

After a Sunday morning Eucharist in Harlem about twenty years ago, a priest told me a woman at the altar rail had refused to take Communion from her and waited instead for the priest who was a white man to offer her Communion. Kneeling at the rail the communicant said she would not take Communion from the "dirty hands" of the black woman priest. Knowing what we know about who tends to wash their hands, I think the woman priest would have been the safer bet, but that aside, her hands were not visibly dirty. We both looked at her hands after the service—turned them over and checked her nails, all good. They looked to me a lot like what I suspect the woman at the rails hands looked like. They looked a lot like mine.

What I am going to write is personal. Women's ordination is both an institutional issue and a personal experience. Many understand the ordination of women to be a reclamation of the earliest forms of church in Acts, an egalitarian model with influential women as early leaders in resistance to the values of empire before the church itself was co-opted by empire. Today, our most senior elected leaders in The Episcopal Church are women. The institution seems to be changing or returning to its roots. Alleluia!

Women's ordination is a radical disruption of privilege in our society. For women of color, a confrontation of both race and gender privilege, for queer or trans women, even more transgression of privilege. That transgression is experienced in bodies, bodies whose dignity is regularly contested.

Whether or not we think we should believe the priesthood should be iconic, the ordination of women illustrates that many of us, low-church and high-church, catholic and evangelical, believe the priesthood is iconic. The priesthood is a glimpse of the Incarnation, a doctrine embodied, and there are bodies whose presentation in that role shocks and maybe even offends us.

And then there is power.

Fourteen years ago, as a soon-to-be transitional deacon, my very first job interview was with the rector from an important progressive beacon of a church who told me that it would be too distracting to have me walking down the aisle every Sunday. I remember being stuck in a car at the very conservative church the deployment officer had insisted I must interview with out of anger that he had to let me interview anywhere, and the associate rector placing his hand firmly on my thigh for a long time to tell me what a pleasure our time together had been. I remember the member of the bishop's staff who when told I would be at a meeting asked me why, would I be dancing on the table for them? I was asked just last week about Timothy's perspective on women in leadership by a troubled visitor at church, and I won't bother you with all of the times I am told how young and articulate I am. Power. It works. I felt humiliated, isolated, and on guard for my safety, not quite the *orans* position.

I know how to have humor. I know how to be disarming or publicly diminish incidents of bigotry. I know how to change the subject and keep going. Sometimes I confront this kind of insult directly. The risk is that the situation becomes about you; a very effective tool of oppression is to shine the light on the one who names it. We live in an interconnected mess of prejudice, and there is a lot of work to do daily to operate under a different paradigm.

I am writing this for all of the women pursuing their vocations in the church and wondering if they are alone in experiences of harassment and degradation from colleagues, supervisors, and parishioners, including the women and people of color. It is tough to know who you can trust with these stories, when we are supposed to be the pastoral ones, listening to other people's difficult stories, not telling our own. You are not the only one. You are not crazy. You are beautiful, articulate, youthful in appearance, and every other putting-you-in-your-place description that they say of you. More importantly, you are a gifted leader, teacher, and pastor. Thank you. There are aspects of the image of Christ emerging in the church through you, and you know how that Jesus thing turns out.

I have heard women's ordination and other acts of inclusion in the church described as an opening up or a breaking down of barriers, creating space for the Holy Spirit. Women's ordination as an unleashing of the power of the Spirit is a powerful image. True in many ways, but maybe not quite enough in thinking through how we do something so countercultural as empower women to lead.

I wonder if the barriers that still stand firm for women in this image of the unleashed Spirit still at times end with the Spirit banging her head against impervious, invisible boundaries, a glass box or cage. Women in many roles and professions in U.S. society are challenged by discrimination, which includes the reluctance of women and men to receive their authority and the belittling of women by the policing of their bodies and self-expression. It should not be surprising, if disappointing, that this same discrimination exists in the church.

The image that comes to mind for me for the embrace of the full inclusion of people not accepted in the church and particularly not into ordained leadership is more like a brace on a weakened limb. I think our society is broken, damaged, and not set up to support itself with equity for all. We need structural support to act differently.

If you are someone or know someone who lives with a physical disability that means your limbs do not work well or you do not have control over them, this image might be especially poignant for you. If you are someone whose mobility or functioning is improved by a medical appliance, it might be a hopeful image.

Here is why I think inclusion in all orders is like a weakened limb or a structurally unsound one that requires a brace. I grew up wearing casts, braces, and eventually orthotics, and when I did not wear them, because what had been so visibly wrong looked under my control or repaired to the adults in my world, I walked in a lot of pain. I limped when I forgot to control how I walked, and I got scolded for not walking correctly by teachers and a society in which "black people shuffled" or so I was told.

I did not understand until I was an adult that some of this was pure and simple racism. I also did not understand that my legs do not work well without support. I knew my feet hurt terribly, and that it felt risky to lift them at times and really tricky to put them down on the ground in the way that everyone else did. What I find interesting about how I thought as a child was that it never occurred to me, that I can recall, to tell anyone my feet hurt. I assumed everybody's feet felt like mine, that we were all learning to walk correctly together. I thought I was just behind in learning to use my feet, but I was pretty good at other things in school, so it would be okay when I finally figured it out.

You can imagine how I felt as a twenty-two-year-old when a doctor first gave me appropriately designed orthotics and the next year when another doctor gave me a prescription for running shoes that had a metal bar in them that held my feet straight. I began to remember other things. I remembered the pictures with my legs in casts. I remembered why I had been sent to India as a baby. I remembered getting fitted for custom shoes as a child. I remembered how much it always hurt to walk. I remembered that I had torn a tendon in my foot as a teenager simply by walking and how suspicious everyone seemed of my explanation.

I started to think of how I had defined my choices in life in relation to how close I would be to a car that I could hop to on one foot, if necessary. I remember the feeling of extreme nausea and dizziness that I thought was about being thin and weak, for which I was tested for anemia. I never thought to mention how badly my feet hurt before one of those episodes.

I think the inclusion of women, people of color, and LGBT people in the ordained leadership of the church is like putting a brace on a weakened limb. We are holding up and supporting a part of the body of the church and society that should not be left to do the best it can on its own. It is an unnecessary pain that only further weakens the body, mind, and spirit of our church. We are a church and society so weakened by millennia of prejudice, so profoundly weakened and maybe even structurally unsound from the beginning, that we would be wise to understand we need a lot of external support, like an exoskeleton: canons; new language; work on inclusivity, like massage, stretching, and focused exercise; daily work, because when we do not, we find ourselves acting out of the anxiety of our repressed histories of pain. Our collective histories are held in the body of the church, from which, with the right support, we might be able to gain new perspectives and healing.

Maybe what we thought was our personal struggle to keep up was something else. Maybe what we thought was an accepted common experience was a sign of sickness. Maybe we have new language and new compassion to develop, and maybe we can spare another generation the pain.

The thing about a weakness in the body like the one I am learning about in myself is that it impacts everything, but we get used to it. If my neck hurts, it would be wise to consider how my feet hit the ground without tendons to support them and some tendons restricting what should happen, and how that impacts every system in my body. I can work out the knots in my shoulder and blame typing with poor posture because that involves some personal responsibility, but I'm pretty much guaranteed that my neck will tighten up again. My back will spasm. My muscles will quit. As much as we might like a more modern, common, or empowered explanation, one that takes personal responsibility like hunching over a computer, if we pay attention, all the symptoms don't really point to that as a cause.

I'm telling you far too much about myself to give you a framework to consider what the impact to the body might be of our deeply embedded prejudices, and how much work we should expect if we are to be as countercultural as I believe we must be in supporting women in leadership.

The week before my induction as rector of St. Mark's in-the-Bowery, our congregation's archivist hesitantly handed me an old manila folder.

It had a faded label on which was typed "Murray, Dr. Pauli." He found it in the archives room of the church, which was primarily filled with old vestry records and fading posters. It was a file of her correspondence with former rectors of St. Mark's and the officers of the General Convention of The Episcopal Church.

I have had a small image of the Reverend Dr. Pauli Murray on the desktop of my computer for the last fifteen years. I'm not sure why. Something about her image as a frail black woman priest in her 60s with great, heavy glasses continues to be moving to me. I am in awe of her legacy as a legal scholar, historian, activist, and writer.

Her story has interrupted mine many times over the years. During my first year at St. Mark's, a man came to my office to ask me to bury his mother. Among his mother's many stories, she had told him once that she had been a house mother at Howard University and was told by the dean of the law school that he was considering admitting a student if she, the house mother for the women's dorm, would be willing to have her live in her residence hall, near the exterior doors. When she asked why someone would be admitted or not based upon their willingness to house her and why near the doors, the dean said her "questionable lifestyle" was the issue. She was rumored to be a lesbian and therefore a risk in a women's dorm. Keith's mother said she would be happy to have her in her residence.

My file at St. Mark's contains an article from the February 11, 1974, *New York Times* that includes this passage: "Dr. Murray has set forth on a new mission. She has enrolled in the General Theological Seminary in hopes of becoming a priest. The Episcopal Church does not ordain women as priests."[30] The Reverend Dr. Pauli Murray, the first African-American woman to be ordained a priest, died in 1989.

In 1989 in my first year in college, I had what felt like a call experience, a deep knowing that I should become a priest. I had no idea what that meant, or if there was such a thing as a woman priest, but I felt a call and planned to file it away for things to think about when I turned forty. I had never met a woman who was a priest. My father says he remembers that Barbara Harris was made bishop that year, and it was on the front page of the Dallas newspapers. I don't remember.

In 1996 I began a Masters of Divinity program at Union Theological Seminary in New York City. I was a postulant for holy orders in the Diocese of Los Angeles. I was attending Union for a variety of reasons, including that the trial of the Right Reverend Walter Righter for heresy was going on at the time, and most Episcopal seminaries were struggling with their policies for how to matriculate and house gay and lesbian students, single and partnered.

My bishop and an undergraduate professor suggested that I might not stick with The Episcopal Church or the ordination pro-cess if I were to attend one of the Episcopal seminaries. I thought they meant that as a person interested in liberation theologies and the early church with an undergraduate degree in religious studies, I might want a deeper dive academically than some of my fellow students. I think they understood more than I thought they would.

---

30 Eleanor Blau, "63 and an Activist, She Hopes to Become an Episcopal Priest," *The New York Times*. February 11, 1974, p. 41.

I know now that they thought I would find the racism, sexism, and homophobia discouraging, possibly discouraging enough not to want to be in those spaces or in this church. As they said, I had other choices.

At the time I took all of their cautions seriously, but I did not think through carefully what they were saying about The Episcopal Church. I had grown up in church: Orthodox, Protestant, and Anglican. I thought I knew how to function within it. I was learning that the Christian church in general was struggling with women in leadership.

I come from a family that is aware of barriers in this country in employment for women and people who are not white. They were careful to guide us toward careers in which technical knowledge and advanced degrees would give someone like me some unquestionable credibility, and if I were really gifted in some area, maybe even the chance to excel. I did not have aspirations to supersede my parent's class location or educational achievement. I shared their goals for me to have the capacity to be financially independent and to make a contribution to society, as they themselves had done. If anything, I thought I was not particularly ambitious or able, yet I was in no way lacking in confidence that I should easily succeed in my modest chosen profession as a priest in the church. I was excited and had tunnel vision while in the ordination process. I was working toward a goal, and it was all-consuming to try to work enough to pay for seminary and get the requirements done, and occasionally done well. I never thought about what it would mean to work as a priest.

I did not understand the function of priestly bodies in sacramental traditions. Intellectually, I did. I wrote about it for class. I did not understand how the audacity of shifting the icon of priest from Northern European to South Asian, from male to female, from old to young would feel. My third year in seminary, my diocese's deployment officer told me I was undeployable. He didn't tell me why. I could guess. I believed him.

The ordination of women of color, all of us—Asian, Pacific Islander, African, Native American, and Latina, cis and trans—unearths deep bias within our communities and the institution and forces a regular confrontation with that bias. It can be funny in its absurdity and extraordinarily painful. In the end, it is redemptive to the institution as the image of priest is broadened to include all kinds of human beings, but it can also be soul crushing to those of us who bring new images and new voices to the table. It is a movement that requires support.

I do not mean to prioritize the role of priests, except that priests in our tradition, for better or for worse, and I think in deeply flawed ways, speak to us about what bodies we value. Who is Christ-like.

I remember, clearly, the first time I saw a woman preside at an altar in an Episcopal church. I was twenty-four years old. It was 1996. I was in St. Mary's Church in West Harlem. She was not someone I knew, and I could not stop crying. It was simply her physical presence, her skin color, her hair, and her voice. She could have prayed to Darth Vader behind that altar, and I would have still wept. The cost to her to fulfill that role was loneliness and insult. It was her hands that were called dirty.

Pauli Murray was a lay leader at St. Mark's in-the-Bowery. She was the first woman on the vestry. She must have been a difficult character because people that were around when she was in the diocese fall silent when I mention her name. She imagined a world of racial equality and integration. She insisted on honoring the integration of races in her own body and the difficult history that made it so. She was iconic in her priesthood as the descendant of slave and slaveholder. Christ like. She did not believe you could separate movements. She was a woman. She was at the strategy table as an attorney when national civil rights cases were being planned, but not the face to present the case. There was the question of her "lifestyle." Some of us are privileged to inherit that mantle, if not the intellect and drive.

In *Proud Shoes: The Story of an American Family*, Pauli Murray tells the story of her grandfather, a man of mixed race who fought in the Civil War and bears unbelievable discrimination and repeated setbacks as he tries with his wife to create a life with simple dignity for his family. He struggles with a condition that caused occasional blindness but had such a drive to live that he would sometimes crawl on the ground through the woods to get himself home when he lost his sight. He insisted upon thriving. Pauli Murray clearly inherited her grandfather's drive to live despite overwhelming barriers with nothing on her side except her Holy Spirit–like drive to survive, educate herself, and improve the state of the world. Not a brace or support in sight.

Some of us have stories like that. I don't. I wore braces and had doctors. At times the nonviolent communication skills I struggle to internalize feel a lot like making my voice nonthreatening enough that people might choose to work with someone who looks like me. I have some intellectual context for the constant suppression and intrusion upon self that women at the altar undergo silently for the privilege of fulfilling vocation. The irony of the situation in this time of institutional decline is not lost to many of us who are the ones renewing congregations ravaged by men who could not imagine what use the church could be in this time.

For you seeking to be faithful to this ministry, whether you are walking proudly or groping along in the dark, we can do this. We can generate support, like the interior of my big, ugly shoes that act like an exoskeleton and make all kinds of flourishing possible. Don't forget. If you take those things off, you cannot walk far, much less run. The pain does not make you stronger. You do not deserve it. We all need to be supported and not just for our own flourishing but so that the church can be who it is called to be.

We've had some of these supports in place for certain men for a long time. No one is able to withstand all that comes at us in these fraught human institutions alone. We are now charged with ensuring that we do not tell another generation that if they try hard enough they could make it look like they were not being hurt in the pursuit of their vocations.

Healing is an unleashing of the Spirit. We can support you on all sides, but the truth-facing, radical work of healing, being well, not whole, is of God. We do all the rest that Christ may be known in our time through the church. May God bless the work of our hands.

THE REVEREND WINNIE VARGHESE is the thirteenth rector of St. Mark's Church in-the-Bowery, the oldest site of continuous worship in New York. St. Mark's is a diverse, energetic, growing congregation in a site on the National Register, partnering with critically acclaimed resident arts partners—Danspace, The Poetry Project, and Incubator Theatre—to engage the community seven days a week. Winnie edited the recently released *What We Shall Become: The Future and Structure of The Episcopal Church*. Winnie has been featured in the teaching series: *Living the Questions 2* and *Via Media*, and has written for *The Witness*, *Episcopal Life*, *The Huffington Post*, and *The Episcopal Journal*. She has served on the Executive Council of The Episcopal Church, the board of the Episcopal Peace Fellowship, Episcopal Divinity School, the Episcopal Evangelical Education Society, and the Episcopal Service Corps. She is a graduate of Southern Methodist University '94 and Union Theological Seminary '99.

CHAPTER 12

Expectation Not Entitlement: Millennial Women Discern Their Place in the Church

Amity Carrubba

Twentysomething women expect women's leadership in the church today. These women, part of the much discussed Millennial generation—those born from the early 1980s to the early 2000s[1]—have grown up in a era of women's leadership, both in the church and throughout American culture. Seeing women in both lay and ordained leadership capacities encourages their involvement in The Episcopal Church. Furthermore, women's leadership is a catalyst for their own commitment to social justice work.

Their expectation for women's leadership perpetuates the reality. Women clergy are not some sought-after dream or goal, but a reality in the lives of many Millennial Episcopalians, both men and women. Seeing ordained women encourages women in their twenties to include ordination alongside other options as they discern a vocation, a primary part of life's work during the development stage of young adulthood. The fact that women leaders are present sets a cultural tone in The Episcopal Church that keeps lifelong Episcopalians and attracts those newer to the denomination.

---

1 Paul Taylor and Scott Keeter, eds., "Millennials: A Portrait of Generation Next," *Pew Research Center* (Feb. 2010): 4 (accessed September 21, 2013).

This expectation is also a tribute to the work and struggle for gender inclusion in The Episcopal Church by countless women and their male allies. For more than fifty years, Episcopalians have fought against the exclusion of women from leadership positions in the church, and their significant strides have created the institution that Millennial women now inherit. The sacrifice of many trail-blazing women provides young adult women today with the ability to choose and take time for more selective discernment.

The expectation for women's leadership in The Episcopal Church is not entitlement. Entitlement is based in selfishness and privilege. It is demanding without doing. Conversely, the expectation of young adult women is marked by their implicit value to the church as well as eagerness to lead and to serve. They assume that they are valued members of the community. They trust that women will be included in all levels of church leadership and that they will be allowed the opportunity to discern their place in the denomination, with all doors and possibilities standing open. Millennial women are hopeful about their full participation and inclusion in The Episcopal Church. They experience *and* envision a church that includes them.

In Service of the Church

One way hundreds of young adults are participating in the life of The Episcopal Church today is serving with Episcopal Service Corps (ESC), the national network of yearlong service programs for recent college graduates sponsored by Episcopal parishes, dioceses, and other denominational institutions. Participants, more than half of whom are women, live in intentional community and serve at nonprofit internships for nine to twelve months. The year of service is often transformative, not only for the corps members but also for the local community in which they serve and for the Episcopal host community.

ESC is in many ways a contemporary expression of a traditional, monastic model of Christian life, although the commitment made is for about a year rather than a lifetime. The communities of twenty-somethings share meals, pray together, and serve the needs of those at the margins in their host cities and towns. Some work with people who are homeless in Los Angeles, some serve in schools in Newark, others work for environmental justice in Fayetteville, Arkansas. The type of service varies across the country, but the processes of confronting and questioning systems of injustice and oppression are consistent. Some participants are discerning a call to ordained ministry; all are discerning their vocations while in direct service or advocacy-related positions. Locating oneself in the nonprofit sector and working to address the world's needs is a unique and particular context. Issues of justice, ministry, liberation, and peace permeate the experience.

I have served as the executive director of ESC since early 2011. My path to this work began in 2000, the year I did a year of service to discern a call to ordained ministry. Although a lifelong Episcopalian, I did not know about the handful of Episcopal young adult yearlong service programs open at the time. Instead, I served with a small Roman Catholic program in Chicago, which introduced me to the church's witness to and action for social justice. My faith and my worldview were forever impacted by the experience. Living in community, struggling to sort out exactly what that meant, and living a vowed life—if only for a year—was deeply formative and felt like the most natural expression of "living" church. My year of service firmly grounded me in my faith and established a deep commitment to Christianity as a way of life that no other experience in the church had done. It helped me claim the faith my family had gifted to me as my own adult faith.

Since many expectations and assumptions have been laid upon the Millennial generation, in both the church and in wider American culture, I was curious to learn what twentysomething Episcopal women thought of women's ordination in the denomination. I wondered what they thought of the legacy as well as what the inclusion of women in all orders of the church might mean in the future, as this generation ages. I spoke with four ESC alumnae: Sarah, JoBeth, Natalie, and Becky, all of them twentysomething Episcopal women who served in ESC programs across the country. We spoke about The Episcopal Church's action around gender equality with the ordination of women and about opening up other leadership positions to women and how those steps relate to ongoing work on other social justice issues today. We also discussed their experience of women's leadership while serving with ESC at their service site or in the program itself. Finally, I asked about their own process of vocational discernment and what it meant to them to have ordained ministry as an option, even if they discerned that it was not how God was calling them to participate in the church and live out their Christian faith.

Sarah's Story

Sarah is the one ESC alumna I spoke with who is seeking ordination in The Episcopal Church. A twenty-four-year-old seminarian at Yale Divinity School, she is a lifelong Episcopalian originally from Alabama. After graduating from Mount Holyoke College in 2011, Sarah stayed in the Northeast for a year of service with Saint Hilda's House, the ESC program in New Haven, Connecticut. Although the church began ordaining women fifteen years before she was born, Sarah believes it is a myth that The Episcopal Church has solved its gender issues. She observed that Episcopalians are more inclined to discuss sexual orientation, race, or other social justice issues than to continue conversations on gender equality. This was true at St. Hilda's House, where corps members were more apt to discuss diversity around sexual orientation and gender identity rather than the church's work on the full inclusion of women. The fact that Alabama, her childhood diocese, sent their first clergywoman deputy to General Convention in 2003 is symbolic of the hurdles to women's leadership that persist in the church, yet it is not the whole story. Sarah is quick to recall how women mentored and encouraged other women in ministry. In particular, the female associate rector at her childhood parish was an important mentor and source of great encouragement early in Sarah's calling to ordination.

Sarah had a mixed experience of women's leadership and the role of women leaders at her service placement, the United Way of Greater New Haven. The ESC internship was Sarah's first job after graduating from college and she wanted a supervisor to mentor and encourage her. Instead, the atmosphere was one where women leaders were there to get the job done, not to offer guidance and encouragement to interns. Sarah observed and learned from various female coworkers' leadership styles. She noticed that some were more motherly or pastoral while others were much more direct and corporate. Sarah began exploring her own leadership style in the midst of these diverse examples.

Many of her United Way coworkers were Roman Catholic. They asked Sarah about ordination of women in The Episcopal Church. They had many questions about how it worked and what it meant for the church to ordain women. Sarah shared how she was called to priestly ministry when she was fourteen years old while attending a Roman Catholic school. It was a mystical experience, beginning years of discernment. With encouragement from her female associate rector, Sarah never questioned women in church leadership; it was a "no-brainer" that women were clergy. Sarah's parents and siblings were also supportive, never questioning her call as a woman. Sarah feels such a strong pull to the priesthood that if The Episcopal Church did not ordain women, she would seriously consider leaving the denomination, or work passionately to change it from within.

Sarah's ESC program is sponsored by Christ Church and program participants are expected to attend and serve in the liturgies. The majority of clergy serving in the parish are men and oftentimes she was the only woman in the sacristy preparing to serve at the altar. This was a difficult adjustment for Sarah, having recently graduated from a college with women in leadership at all levels and having been mentored by clergywomen in both Alabama and Western Massachusetts. Sarah recognized her desire to have female colleagues even in the midst of supportive male clergy in the parish and in the ESC program.

The "old boys club" is still alive and well in parts of The Episcopal Church and there are many places where clergywomen are absent, new, or at best simply underrepresented. This frustrates Sarah since the denomination claims female clergy. That said, clergywomen serve and lead in many corners of The Episcopal Church. What's more, many female and male church leaders encourage and mentor Millennial women into leadership. It is important to recognize that both realities exist in order to cultivate a more gender equal denomination. If Episcopalians assume work for gender justice is complete, we shall fall short. If we focus only on the distance yet to go, we shall devalue accomplishments already achieved. As a Millennial and committed Episcopalian, Sarah is inspired by both the inclusion of women to date and the work still remaining. She is passionate about cultivating a church where no one is unsure of his or her place in the faith community based on their gender, color, sexual orientation, or gender expression.

JoBeth's Story

JoBeth came to The Episcopal Church only a few years ago, while in college. Raised Southern Baptist, the twenty-three-year old served with The Julian Year, the ESC program in Chicago, for two consecutive years beginning in 2012. Her experience of women's leadership in the Southern Baptist tradition was limited to women leading Sunday school and organizing potlucks. While studying at Oklahoma Baptist University, it was clear to JoBeth that she wanted to go into ministry. She started her studies as a youth ministry major with a minor in Bible. There were other women in her classes, yet everyone—male and female, students and professors—assumed they could not be pastors in the church. The role of women in church leadership was often a controversial topic among students who either majored or minored in Bible. A professor asked JoBeth about her thoughts on women's leadership in the church after she wrote a paper on the portrayal of wisdom as feminine in Proverbs. By that time JoBeth had started attending an Episcopal parish in the community and began to assume that women's voices had authority in the church. Eventually, she found her way to Episcopal Service Corps. It was inspiring for JoBeth to see clergywomen at Diocesan Convention and in parishes, particularly because she had come from a tradition that did not accept women in leadership.

JoBeth identified a connection between gender justice work and being better able to be in solidarity with other marginalized groups. JoBeth observed that a group of people is better able to empathize with other groups through its own journey to justice. Working for one's own justice encourages thinking outside the "box of privilege" according to JoBeth. If it is assumed that women are equal, it leads other groups of people who are marginalized to work for and expect equality.

When coworkers and clients at JoBeth's service placement, Connections for the Homeless, learned that she was serving with Episcopal Service Corps, they often assumed she was in the ordination process. She did not know if her coworkers and clients already knew that The Episcopal Church regularly ordains women, or if they assumed the denomination ordained women because they viewed JoBeth's service as the work of the church. Either way, they not only assumed that ordination was an option in general, but JoBeth's future in particular. Needless to say, this surprised her given her Southern Baptist upbringing. JoBeth realized she had a responsibility in leadership, which was significant for her personally.

Most of JoBeth's coworkers at Connections for the Homeless were women, so it was a given that women were leaders at her service placement. This was an encouraging change, since she had witnessed women professors and administrators passed over for promotions and prominent positions of leadership at her university.

JoBeth's understanding of her own leadership grew from her experience serving in an organization with many women leaders. She learned how to lead, in particular when to stand her ground and when to let things go, from women at the nonprofit.

JoBeth considered ordination very briefly but decided against it. Having ordination as an option, while going through a time of intentional vocational discernment, was important to her. In her experience, simply having the option "on the table" affected the culture in which she was trying to discern her vocation and how she thought about her own discernment. The message JoBeth heard through her ESC experience was that The Episcopal Church was willing to welcome her, walk with her, and accept her where she was in her faith journey.

Natalie's Story

Women's leadership was very present and important during Natalie's year of service. Originally from Kansas, she moved to Boston in 2011 for a year of service a year after graduating from Kansas State University. Almost all the staff at Natalie's service placement, the afterschool program at St. Steven's Episcopal Church, were women—from the rector to her direct supervisor. Furthermore, about half the leaders of Life Together, the ESC program in which Natalie served, were female priests. It was evident to Natalie that supporting women clergy and women's leadership in general was important not only in Life Together, but throughout the Diocese of Massachusetts and in Episcopal Service Corps. In the twenty-six-year-old's opinion, this was a very good dynamic for the program as well as for her personally.

Throughout her year of service, Natalie was exposed to different women's leadership styles—from motherly to more authoritative. This encouraged her to explore her own leadership and to try out different styles. Natalie commented how she has never felt called to ordained ministry, but many people have asked her about it, based on her involvement in the church. When people see her potential, it reinforces the fact to Natalie that her role in the church and her leadership are not limited by her gender.

Although not seeking ordination herself, Natalie has women friends her age who are in the ordination process in various dioceses across the county. She notices subtle differences in the ordination processes for women and believes these differences reveal how some dioceses are more supportive and others less supportive of women in the process. Gender bias is not often recognized today, according to Natalie, yet she understands the bias is still present. She noted how Episcopalians tend to forget that gender is still a real dynamic in the church, even though many have moved their focus to LGBT equality. Ultimately, Natalie sees the church's work around gender equality as intimately linked to other social justice issues and believes that working on one issue supports and encourages equality and inclusion for others. Luckily, she knows she does not have to compartmentalize her justice work as a member of The Episcopal Church, which is one reason she remains committed to the denomination.

Becky's Story

Becky served with Episcopal Service Corps because The Episcopal Church ordains women. She served with The Julian Year in Chicago for two years after graduating from The University of North Carolina at Chapel Hill because the female associate rector at her home church encouraged her. More than that is the reality that Becky, age twenty-five, may not have remained in The Episcopal Church if women were not accepted into all orders and levels of leadership.

The church's work around gender justice in Becky's lifetime has shaped a culture that engages and inspires her—working for inclusive justice in the church community enables the church to work for inclusive justice in the world. She observes, "You can't fix things until you fix yourself; you cannot help others until you help yourself." Although the church is still striving for justice and peace among all people, and working to respect the dignity of every human being, Becky's commitment is to a church committed to justice for all people.

Many leaders at Becky's service placement, Holy Family Ministries School, were women—including the president and the principal. The entire staff in the administration office and a majority of the teachers were women. Although Becky was in an environment full of women, one woman in particular inspired Becky at her service placement. The principal of the school began her career as a nurse but later went back to school and completed a master's degree in education. She was a great inspiration to Becky for her perseverance in changing career paths and for her sustained dedication to the students and school community. The program director of The Julian

Year, a clergywoman, affirmed Becky's interest in nonprofit work and is part of the reason Becky is now pursuing a graduate degree in nonprofit management. The program director also offered incredible pastoral presence to Becky throughout her two years of service.

Serving with ESC changed Becky's understanding of ordained ministry. A lifelong Episcopalian, she came into the program holding assumptions about clergy being without flaws or doubts. The year of service changed her perception and made her admire ordained ministry even more. She often explored questions about what a calling to ordained ministry looks like through intense conversations with fellow participants in The Julian Year. Becky observed that it was meaningful to each of her peers—female and male—to be free to ask if they felt called to ordained ministry while engaging the larger question: What am I meant to do with my life?

Freedom in Discernment

Young adult women are the beneficiaries of a seismic shift in Episcopal Church leadership. They have come to expect that which they have already been a witness to, that which has permeated their experience of The Episcopal Church and larger American culture since birth. A parallel may be made with this generation's experience of technology. As "digital natives,"[2] this generation has grown up with unprecedented access to technology. Most do not recall when they first learned how to use a computer or a video game controller. Technology has simply always been a part of life, an *integral* part at that. Similarly, many Millennials are also "native" recipients of ordained women's leadership in The Episcopal Church, not having known the denomination before women were ordained, always being in a church that ordained women, or having women clergy baptize them.

The inclusion of women's leadership in The Episcopal Church permeates the culture in which young adult women have grown up. In church, in government, in corporations, women have served at the highest levels since Millennial women can remember. This is not to say or assume such leadership has come easily or without great effort. Young women have also grown up hearing about glass

---

2 Marc Prensky,"Digital Natives, Digital Immigrants," *On the Horizon* 9, no. 5 (2001): 1 (accessed September 21, 2013).

ceilings, although perhaps this is more often discussed in reference to government or corporations than the church.

Having the freedom to wonder and explore how a person knows they are called to ordained ministry and what role doubt might play in discernment was important for Sarah, JoBeth, Natalie, and Becky in their personal process of discernment. Including ordination as an option alongside numerous other possible vocational paths made the process more complete. In fact, having the option to discern an ordained call reinforced the reality that their role and leadership capacity in The Episcopal Church was not limited by their gender. It was meaningful for the church to say "you can do this too" even if they discerned a call to serve in the church as a laywoman.

Many women, and men for that matter, serving with ESC are discerning a call to ordained ministry. The opportunity to serve in the church while discerning is one reason a year of service with ESC is attractive to many young adults. Millennial women are part of the so-called "third wave" of American feminism. While many begin ESC with thoughts about ordained ministry, they are in many ways freer than previous generations of Episcopal women to discern both lay and ordained leadership. Young adult women are not as bound to the institutional church structures that often push toward ordination, which in turn allows each woman the freedom to pursue her vision of justice and service in a wider variety of contexts. This freedom may be a reflection of greater acceptance and validity of lay service alongside ordained service in the Millennial generation or a unique contribution of third-wave feminism.

As Millennial women mature into leadership positions in the church and in the world, how do they take on the mantle? Many of these women ask where else the church is working for justice and authentic diversity—not simply diversity, but full inclusion. The Episcopal Church's action around gender equality, in part through the ordination of women, creates a beneficial chain reaction leading to deeper, wider, larger inclusion of other previously marginalized groups. Young adult women expect women's leadership—both lay and ordained—in The Episcopal Church and ask who else is still left outside the beloved community. They are neither satisfied with their own "piece of the leadership pie," nor are they satisfied with gender justice as thus far achieved in the church, however imperfectly, but desire and expect justice for all.

Photos from the Past, A Glimpse into the Future

Photographs of vestries from decades past consisting of white men posing for the camera in three-piece suits have adorned the walls and archives of most of the parishes where I have been, either as lay member or clergy. Often the counterparts to these photos also appear, those of women's guilds having organized teas in the undercroft. You must be diligent in a search for photographs of the first woman on the vestry or the first female warden, if photo documentation of these early leaders exists at all. Evidence of the first female deacons and priests, first female General Convention deputies, first female bishops, first female presiding bishop, or first female president of the House of Deputies is often easier to come by, perhaps because these positions are by nature more public. Either way, the leadership of women in The Episcopal Church is well established alongside that of men throughout much of the denomination. Young adult women today do not question whether they may or have the capacity to serve in these roles; instead these women have the space for real discernment. Furthermore, they often need not worry about the impact of declining a leadership role as a woman, because there are likely other women who will serve. Millennial women can expect that they will have not only female peers, but also older female mentors to guide them as they take on leadership roles in the church. It will be exciting to observe how women's involvement in justice work and ministry will impact the life and mission of The Episcopal Church in the decades to come as the Millennial generation matures.

THE REVEREND AMITY CARRUBBA grew up in the Episcopal Church and in an Air Force family. After moving ten times across the United States and Europe, she now lives and works in the Chicago area. Originally pursuing a career in pharmaceutical research, Amity took a leap of faith in 2000 to participate in a young adult service program. The experience was life-changing and led to a call to ordained ministry. Since graduation from Episcopal Divinity School and ordination in 2006, Amity has served three parishes and currently serves as executive director of Episcopal Service Corps, an Episcopal nonprofit organization. Amity enjoys international travel, watching documentaries, and listening to the blues.

CHAPTER 13

Toward an "Irregular" Embrace: The Philadelphia Ordinations and Transforming Ideas of the Human

Cameron Partridge

In October 1991, as a first-year student at Bryn Mawr, a small, liberal arts women's college in Pennsylvania, I stumbled upon *Womanpriest*, Alla Bozarth Campbell's 1978 memoir of her experience as one of the "Philadelphia Eleven," the first women ordained to the priesthood in The Episcopal Church. A commemorative plate revealed that the book was a gift of Jeanette Piccard, class of 1918, who was also ordained that hot summer day in July 1974. I had known we had women priests, and that this fact was still controversial in some quarters. I was also aware that we had gay and lesbian clergy, and had been captivated a few months earlier by a brief story and photo of the Reverend Elizabeth Carl in *Time* magazine.[1] What was this story of discernment and daring, of collective action and negotiation, of an exuberant liturgy that had irrupted into the church of my childhood, and taken place just a few miles from my college? As one whose bursting into feminist consciousness the previous year had complicated an emerging sense of call to priesthood, I had to drop everything and devour this tale. Immediately heading to my room, I read it, refracting my own questions in and through it.

---

1 Richard Ostling, "What Does God Really Think About Sex?: Christians of All Sorts Are Battling Over the Issues of Homosexuality, Infidelity, and Fornication," *Time* (June 24, 1991): 48–50.

Through *Womanpriest* and, later, Carter Heyward's 1976 memoir *A Priest Forever,* I encountered a key moment of upheaval and transformation in my ecclesial family history, an event that helped explain unspoken dynamics in which I had long been steeped. I was particularly intrigued by the "irregularity" of the event, a reference to its lack of authorization either by the bishops or the standing committees of the women's own dioceses. To many of its critics, this "irregularity" indicated its "invalidity." To its participants and proponents, its "irregularity" signaled its Spirit-driven, transformative character. To me, returning to narratives of the event forty years after its occurrence and twenty-three years after my library discovery, this "irregularity" reads as an outward and visible sign of an inward and ongoing transformation of our theology of the human.

Indeed, in overlapping yet often compartmentalized waves, the church has long wrestled with its theology of the human through axes of difference, particularly race, class, gender, and sexuality. These facets of humanity seem "irregular" to, and in a sense destabilize and *deregulate,* an upper middle class, white, heterosexual male norm. The editors of *Male and Female . . . Sexuality,* a volume prepared in advance of the 1976 General Convention ordination debates, noted how the subject prompted "deep questions about our understanding of what it is to be human."[2] In what follows I focus on what I am calling "gender irregularity" in the church's struggle over the Philadelphia ordinations. I also point toward a connection between the stigma associated with "gender irregularity" and the complicated early relationship between the movements for women's ordination and those for gay and lesbian equality within The Episcopal Church. Finally, I see in "gender irregularity" a key link between these struggles and the church's most recent steps in support of transgender Episcopalians.

Bending the Binary: "Gender Irregularity"

With this phrase, "gender irregularity," I signal how the norms or expectations of gender were being transgressed or subverted by the first women priests simply because they were taking up a vocation

---

2 Ruth Tiffany Barnhouse and Urban T. Holmes, III, ed., *Male and Female: Christian Approaches to Sexuality* (New York: Seabury Press, 1976), ix.

that had been the sole preserve of men. The system of norms that were being challenged by the women's ordinations is, as feminism of the "third wave" tends to term it, the "gender binary." In evangelical and Roman Catholic language, it is often termed gender or sexual "complementarity." This concept also provides the gendered underpinnings of "heteronormativity"—the idea that heterosexuality should be morally normative. Simply put, this system operates simultaneously on the levels of sex, gender, and sexuality, and asserts:

a) (Biological) Sex: one is born and remains for life either male or female,

b) Gender: if born male, one is expected to be "masculine" and if born female, to be "feminine," and

c) Sexuality: a man is expected to sexually partner with a woman, and vice versa, primarily for purposes of procreation.

At the root of this chain of associations is the idea that women and men form an opposite and heterosexually complementary binary, ultimately asymmetric and patriarchal, weighted in men's favor. This pattern is often asserted to be universal, unchanging, and natural. Yet deviations from this schema—including failing to be appropriately masculine or feminine, failing to marry the "opposite" sex, or failing to marry at all—reveal it as contextually contingent, ambiguous, and unstable. By challenging this asymmetric, privileged access to priesthood, the women were essentially setting off the binary seismograph, destabilizing the distinctions between men and women, as well as the church's broader understandings of the human person. To borrow a phrase from Kate Bornstein, these women were "gender outlaws."[3] But destabilizing the binary itself was not necessarily anyone's intent. Indeed, part of how the ecclesial system coped with the anxiety unleashed by this "gender irregularity" was to seek to stabilize this system once more, to incorporate the binary within the priesthood itself. I believe this anxiety-based response continues to inflect our ecclesial conversations about the human person to this day.

---

3 Kate Bornstein, *Gender Outlaw: On Men, Women, and the Rest of Us* (New York: Vintage Books, 1995).

Race, Class, and Ecclesial Turbulence

The reverberations of 1974 emerged from an already wobbling context. The same 1973 Convention that had failed to authorize women priests had also moved away from the massive General Convention Special Program (GCSP) of 1967, leaving the ongoing church-wide conversation on race and class in a tense, unresolved state.[4] These uncertain dynamics, in which the Church of the Advocate risked hosting the ordinations, contributed further to the event's "irregularity." As the church's rector Paul Washington put it, "a black priest in an aided parish had disobeyed his bishop, the presiding bishop, and the General Convention in an action that was broadcast to the world. I was in trouble."[5] This individual and collective vocation to holy trouble-making was sustained by a strong sense of solidarity across axes of difference.

Women Priests and "Gender Irregularity"

For some, women's entry into male vocational territory rendered them Trojan horses, implicitly destabilizing the identities of the men in their ranks. One of the male clergy who read a statement of protest at the Philadelphia ordinations referred to the event as attempting "to make stones into bread." In the end, he continued, the ordination could only "offer up the smell and sight and sound of perversion."[6] Reading these ordinations through the lens of Jesus's demonic temptation, this expression of misogyny portrayed the women's priestly ordination as both an intrusion into a male domain and a deeply stigmatized category confusion.

Carter Heyward's *A Priest Forever* memorably defines the quandary the first women priests faced at the epicenter of this churchquake. In those earliest days, Heyward explains, "the PRIEST = MAN equation" formed "a catch-22." The first women priests were

---

4 Gardiner Shattuck, *Episcopalians and Race: Civil War to Civil Rights* (Lexington: University Press of Kentucky, 2000); Shattuck, "A Whole Priesthood: The Philadelphia Ordinations (1974) and the Continuing Dilemmas of Race in the Episcopal Church." *Episcopal Divinity School Occasional Papers* (April 2001).

5 Paul M. Washington, *"Other Sheep I Have": The Autobiography of Father Paul M. Washington* (Philadelphia, PA: Temple University Press, 1994), 171.

6 "Eleven Women Ordained Priests," *Diocesan Press Service,* July 31, 1974, The Archives of the Episcopal Church, http://www.episcopalarchives.org/cgi-bin/ ENS/ENSpress_release.pl?pr_number=74200 (accessed November 1, 2013).

more likely to be "strong" and "aggressive" to have the mettle for this early battle. A man with such qualities "would have been welcomed long ago by ecclesiastical authorities," but a woman with such qualities got perceived as "acting like a man." While sporting pants and a relatively short haircut, Heyward received a comment from a male priest, "I want women priests to be real women, not to cut their hair short and wear pants. . . . By the way, I wasn't referring to you!" Clearly "only 'real women,' if any at all," could be ordained. Yet if "real woman" meant being "compliant, undemanding, sweet," they "would not be a likely aspirant to a vocation in which women cannot long manifest 'sugar and spice and everything nice.'" Indeed, another priest commented to Heyward, "I really can't stand to see some of the women deacons running around in short skirts. How do you girls expect us fellows to concentrate on the Lord!" Heyward's canny assessment—"I looked at him and wondered how much time he spent concentrating on the Lord"—highlights the utter absurdity of the women's position. They couldn't win: either they were read as too masculine (and thus men wannabes) or too feminine (and thus sexualized distractions to men). In those early days, a woman priest had to make her way "in a Church in which her gender made her, at best, a curiosity piece and, at worst, an abnormal intruder into male space."[7] No matter what they did, the first women priests were always being judged as "gender irregular."

Amid this catch-22, women came under enormous pressure to dissociate their vocations from men and masculinity and to perform their priesthood in an unambiguously (though not too) feminine register. In *Womanpriest,* Alla Bozarth remarks on repeatedly receiving "the preposterous question, 'Do we call you Father?'" With exasperation she remarks, "I haven't changed my sex or renounced my femaleness by assuming a way of life formerly identified with males. I've merely expanded that way of life—and redefined it—by bringing femaleness to it, by fulfilling the human qualifications for priesthood *as a woman.*" The earliest women priests were part of a broad transformation of what it might mean to be a woman, which in turn was expanding the idea of the human itself. So deeply did this vocational expansion challenge previous ideas of womanhood

---

7 Carter Heyward, *A Priest Forever: The Formation of a Woman and a Priest* (New York: Harper and Row, 1976), 20–21, 32.

that it seemed necessary for Bozarth to state she had not changed her sex. Even as she warded off outside hostilities, she had to confront their internal reverberations. She reports worrying about "unconsciously imitat[ing]" the "tone and mannerisms" of male colleagues, and frequently asking herself, "Am I copying a male stereotype inappropriately, or am I creating ministry out of this unique situation and relationship?"[8] In a context where women were regularly being misunderstood and misrecognized, they wanted to avoid fulfilling the stereotypes others had for them.

At the same time, both the stereotypes and their avoidance continued to render "gender irregularity" as a stigma to be avoided by priests of all genders and sexualities. Particularly in those early days, being a woman priest required not simply being a woman and developing what it might mean to be a woman priest. It also required a performance of gender or gender positioning, a clerical femininity that specifically signaled *not being or desiring to be a man*. It meant *counteridentifying*—to use Jose Esteban Muñoz's term—with men.[9] Further, inasmuch as men were seen as the sole appropriate performers of masculinity, women priests were also under pressure to counteridentify not simply with men but also with any form of masculinity, a distinction to which I will return below. This counteridentification complicated the relationship between the movements for women's and gay and lesbian equality in the church.

"Gender Irregularity" and Sexuality

This complication became particularly visible as Ellen Barrett was ordained to the priesthood in the Diocese of New York in 1978. An openly lesbian woman, Barrett embodied the crossroads of sexuality and gender at a time when the women's ordination movement was seeking to avoid associations with homosexuality. In the wider women's movement, this was the era in which the well-known feminist Betty Friedan had referred to lesbians as a "lavender menace," prompting communal teach-ins about the systemic connections between patriarchy and homophobia. As Caro Hall reports in *A Thorn*

---

8 Alla Bozarth Campbell, *Womanpriest: A Personal Odyssey* (New York: Paulist Press, 1978), 167 (Italics in original, and 170.
9 Jose Esteban Muñoz, *Disidentifications: Queers of Color and the Performance of Politics* (Minnesota: University of Minnesota Press, 1999).

in the Flesh, the Episcopal Women's Caucus declined to deliver a message of support sent to them by the board of Integrity, the LGBT Episcopal organization founded in 1974.[10] Barrett later editorialized in Integrity's newsletter that conservative activists were accusing straight women "of 'cosmic lesbianism,' of trying to subvert and 'lesbianize' the Church."[11] As long as that association dominated the wider ecclesial imagination, the women's movement would be under pressure by the wider church to dissociate itself from homosexuality.

The association of the women's ordination movement with lesbianism (cosmic or otherwise) came from a lingering association between homosexuality and the transgression of gender norms. Because any violation of the gender binary has a way of setting off the seismograph across the levels of sex, gender, and sexuality, "gender irregularity" can tend to be read as a sign of "sexual irregularity"— more specifically of homosexuality. As a result, even as butch/femme identity categories were being strongly critiqued within lesbian communities as examples of "male identification," internalized misogyny, and homophobia, wider heterosexual cultures continued to stereotype lesbians as "mannish." Indeed, Bishop Paul Moore admitted as much in his description of his first meeting with Ellen Barrett: "I suppose I had unconsciously stereotyped the person I would meet: someone in masculine clothes, or dressed in a Greenwich Village kind of outfit . . . a rather militant, even aggressive person who would put me immediately on the defensive."[12] Moore hastened to reassure the reader that Barrett was nothing of the sort. He went on to face tremendous criticism for ordaining her.

Thus in a context where "priest = man," where a woman doing "men's work" = "mannish," and where "mannish" = lesbian, women priests of all sexual orientations were under pressure to avoid anything that might smack of "mannishness." Within this pressure-cooker context, and within the trends of the "second-wave" feminism of the day, there was no space for a woman priest to enact her gender anywhere along the continuum of what Jack Halberstam

---

10 Caroline J. Addington Hall, *A Thorn in the Flesh: How Gay Sexuality Is Changing the Episcopal Church* (Lanham, MD: Rowman & Littlefield Publishers, 2013), 50.

11 Ellen Barrett, "A Letter from the Editor," *Integrity: Gay Episcopal Forum,* May 1975. Quoted in Hall, *Thorn in the Flesh,* 50n17, 261.

12 Paul Moore, Jr., *Take a Bishop Like Me* (New York: Harper & Row, 1979), 42.

has termed "female masculinity," should she feel so called.[13] How she enacted her gender necessarily had to be within a register of femininity further influenced by upper middle class, white expectations of "professional" dress and demeanor. In the early years, the pressure for women priests to counteridentify with "gender irregularity" extended to homosexuality, complicating the interface between these two ecclesial movements. As efforts for gay and lesbian equality in the church emerged amid the movement for women's ordination, the pressure to counteridentify with gender nonconformity continued to build. Not only did this wider context push lesbian women not to perform "gender irregularity," but gay men were also expected to be "straight-acting," indistinguishable from heterosexual men.[14]

"Gender Irregularity" and Transgender

Amid this complex interface, both the women's and the gay and lesbian liberation movements of the 1970s were also actively distancing themselves from the transgender community, the community most closely associated with "gender irregularity." Although gender non-conforming people—trans women, drag queens, butch women—had played key roles in the Stonewall riots, the gay liberation movement that sprang from it increasingly kept the trans community at bay. Concern emerged that gay and lesbian political and legal gains might be hampered by association with those who undertook gender transition or who expressed their gender in transgressive ways. While homosexuality had been removed from the *Diagnostic and Statistical Manual of Mental Disorders* in 1973, Gender Identity Disorder (the diagnosis underlying transsexuality) was added to the *Manual's* next edition in 1980. In the 1970s transgender people also became subject to strong scrutiny from some feminist theorists (especially Mary Daly and her student Janice Raymond). Frequently, trans men (those who transitioned from female to male) were judged traitors who had succumbed to internalized misogyny and homophobia, while trans women (male to female) were read as interlopers in and colonizers of women's space. In an era when the taboos associated with medical transition and

---

13 Judith "Jack" Halberstam, *Female Masculinity* (Durham, NC: Duke University Press, 1998).

14 See, for example, David Halperin, *One Hundred Years of Homosexuality* (New York: Routledge, 1990).

gender transgression continued to multiply, trans people were—and continue to be—stigmatized for their "gender irregularity."[15] Indeed, over the last decade, even as many community fault lines have dissipated, as fresh models of analysis have developed and new modes of identity and embodiment have emerged, trans people continue to face profound, multipronged, systemic violence. This is particularly the case for trans women of color.

Embracing Gender "Irregularity"

In 1991, when I first learned of the Philadelphia ordinations, both my gender and vocational trajectories began to converge in new ways. I became inspired by how the "irregular" spirit of the event helped spur a process of engagement and transformation in the church's understanding of gender, of systems of oppression, and of the human. This spirit stayed with me as I came out as gay in early 1993, and then as transgender in 2001 before being ordained to the priesthood in 2005. During my ordination process in the Diocese of Massachusetts, I longed for trans companions on the way—a Massachusetts Eleven, I joked. Before long, TransEpiscopal, a community of transgender Episcopalians and allies began to form online, becoming a forum for solidarity, shared stories, and eventually of strategic planning. Lay and ordained, we learned we were not alone. Working with allied organizations, such as IntegrityUSA, the Consultation, the Chicago Consultation, we sought to work intersectionally and in coalition. At church-wide gatherings from the 2008 Lambeth Conference Fringe Festival to the General Conventions of 2006, 2009, and 2012, we sought to bear witness to our lives and ministries in the church's ongoing inquiry into the theology of the human person.

As a result of this combined, communal witness, thirty-eight years after the Philadelphia ordinations, the General Convention of The Episcopal Church passed legislation in July 2012 that unambiguously bars discrimination against transgender people at all levels of the church's life. Resolutions D002 and D019 took up two terms that have become crucial to trans legal work in recent years: "gender identity" and "gender expression." Gender identity refers to the gender with which one "identifies," i.e., the internal sense of one's gender.

---

15 See Susan Stryker, *Transgender History* (Berkeley, CA: Seal Press, 2008).

Gender expression indicates how one enacts that internal sense of gender through mannerisms, choice of dress, haircut, makeup, pattern of speech, etc. These additions to the canons (Title III, Canon 1, Sec. 2 and Title 1.17.5) were undeniably a watershed moment. Through this historic vote, The Episcopal Church joined the United Church of Christ as a mainline Christian denomination that officially embraces transgender membership and leadership.

Yet these canonical changes do not simply refer to transgender people who transition from female to male and from male to female. This language should not simply apply to trans men like myself who are read as unambiguously masculine and heterosexual. It does not simply address trans people. It applies to everyone. Ultimately, the deepest significance of this vote is its application to all who do not conform to gender norms, regardless of their gender identity. This canonical change should embolden us to eradicate the stigma of "gender irregularity" in our communities. It should honor women and men who expand expectations of femininity and masculinity, and who embody the truth implicitly proclaimed by the Philadelphia ordinations: there is no *one* way to be a woman or a man. It should open our church to the reality that some of us do not identify as strictly female or male, whether because we were born intersex—biologically neither fully male or female—or because the idea of the gender binary fails to capture the complexity of our lives and identities.[16] It should prompt us to explore more deeply how gender norms vary between and within cultures, and are deeply imprinted by socioeconomic class.

Now, at the fortieth anniversary of the Philadelphia ordinations, our inquiries into the human have in a sense come full circle. In the church and in the world, we now have the opportunity to engage afresh with more liminal, ambiguous, and transforming understandings of gender, always unfolding in concert with various axes of difference. Finally, we are invited to embrace fully the "irregular" spirit of the Philadelphia ordinations. May that embrace deepen and enrich our conception of the human and, ultimately, our membership in the wider body of Christ.

---

16 On intersex and the theology of the human, see Susannah Cornwall, *Sex and Uncertainty in the Body of Christ: Intersex Conditions and Christian Theology* (Sheffield, UK: Equinox, 2010).

THE REVEREND DR. CAMERON PARTRIDGE is the Episcopal chaplain at Boston University and a lecturer and denominational counselor for Episcopal/Anglican Students at Harvard Divinity School. An openly transgender man, Cameron was ordained a priest in the Episcopal Diocese of Massachusetts in 2005, and completed his ThD in 2008. He has served in parish, young adult, and campus ministry contexts. He attended the Lambeth Conference Fringe Festival in 2008, and the General Conventions of 2009 and 2012. In 2013 he was appointed to the A050 Task Force on the Study of Marriage. Cameron is also a husband and a dad—he and his spouse have two young sons.

CHAPTER 14

But We Thought We Were So Normative!: A Male Perspective on Women, Authority, and the Church

Gary Hall

As I look back forty years after the Philadelphia ordinations of 1974, I find the invitation to make sense of that event and the ensuing years of church leadership exercised by women irresistible. It is possible to frame or explain the experience in so many ways. Was it an expression of American feminism? A continuation of the civil rights movement? A theological and missional imperative? All or none of the above?

The discussion over the impact of the ordination of women on church leadership is very much like the debate about climate change that happens after every megastorm. While we can see some large trends, it is hard to ascribe particular changes to any one leader or her ministry. Individuals have a way of being maddeningly idiosyncratic, so perhaps just this once it is excusable to speak in general, not specific, terms.

One way in which I have come to understand this history is to look at it as defined by a tension between two principles. On the one hand we have an American notion of civil equality—familiar to all of us from the civil rights movement, the press for marriage equality, and other contemporary justice causes. As Americans we are committed to the principle of equality under the law. A church that limits its ordained authority to (straight) men presents an obvious violation of that principle.

On the other hand we Christians share a missional imperative to express the fullness of the body of Christ in our community life and a concomitant demand that our ministry reflect the (ethnic, racial, gender, sexual orientation) diversity of the people of God. We believe God is doing in and through us something new, something that transcends our contingent human categories. A church whose leadership is segregated by gender, race, or sexual orientation obviously violates that principle as well.

So in the mid-twentieth century many in the church found that these twin violations of our Christian and American values placed The Episcopal Church in an untenable position. The history leading up to the 1974 Philadelphia ordinations has been well rehearsed, but for the purposes of this essay we need to recall the moral and theological agony that made dramatic action necessary. Rather quickly thereafter, the church regularized those ordinations and opened the process to women nationally, and despite predictions of disaster the whole American church has continued to ordain women bishops, priests, and deacons and call them into the highest ranks of ecclesial authority.

In what follows, I want to reflect a bit on my own working life in the church—as parish priest, seminary and cathedral dean, participant in diocesan and national church life—as it has been informed by both the Philadelphia ordinations of 1974 and my subsequent collegial relationships with women clergy and lay leaders. Everything I say below is anecdotal and unscientific, but it is as true as I can make it to my understanding of my own limited experience.

My working life in The Episcopal Church has been coextensive with the ordination of women to the priesthood and episcopate. I was between my first and second years as a student at Episcopal Divinity School in Cambridge, Massachusetts, when the Philadelphia ordinations took place in 1974. As a student at one of the hotbeds of the women's ordination movement, I spent my seminary years not only caught up in that cause but more importantly studying and working collegially with women from around the United States. When I was ordained to the priesthood in 1977, one of my fellow ordinands (Victoria Hatch) was the first woman ordained a priest in the Diocese of Los Angeles.

Because EDS brought Carter Heyward and Suzanne Hiatt on to the faculty soon after the 1974 ordinations, I also had opportunities not shared by many of my male colleagues at other seminaries in those days—to be taught by ordained Anglican women, to see them preside and preach in chapel, to go to them for professional guidance and pastoral care. We men who studied at EDS in the 1970s thus have a different perspective (I believe) on the ordination and leadership of women than do many of our peers who studied in the same era. Because we experienced women in ecclesial and academic authority in seminary, it was entirely natural for us to accept their authority in the working world of the church. Consequently, we were able to work easily beside women clergy in the lived reality of church life over the course of our careers. I don't mean here to sugarcoat the process—many male seminarians and clergy were hostile and vindictive over the years, especially as women moved into positions of power. And even at EDS in the 1970s there were students and faculty who were for the ordination of women "in principle" but who opposed "irregular" women priests presiding in chapel. But overall the EDS experience helped me and other men clergy forge alliances with our women colleagues as we made our way into the working life of the church.

When EDS decided to hire Carter and Sue soon after the Philadelphia ordinations, the school became the focus for a lot of anger from around the church, and some bishops actually pulled their students out. (It was one thing to ordain women irregularly, another to actually give them jobs. The ongoing ordination-deployment conundrum is for another essay.) Because the school felt itself (and its students) to be in jeopardy, the faculty called a community meeting in the fall of 1974 to discuss all the ramifications of Carter and Sue joining them with full responsibilities to preach and preside in the chapel.

One of the most compelling conversations I ever heard about the Philadelphia ordinations took place that night. Don Colenback, who taught ethics at EDS, argued that the Philadelphia ordinations were yet another case of Christians acting through conscience in civil disobedience. Harvey Guthrie, EDS dean, responded that those ordinations went forward not primarily as a protest but rather as a witness of radical faithfulness to the logic of the gospel. One way to see our actions was as a breaking of canon law as a protest. The other was to understand them as radical obedience to the theology which canon law ultimately exists to serve.

Civil disobedience or radical faithfulness? In some ways, that tension has defined the last forty or so years in the life and ministry of The Episcopal Church. Because the Philadelphia ordinations presented the church with the reality of women priests that its theology could not deny, Anglicanism in America has subsequently found itself defined by both that movement and the presence of women at every level of church leadership. As we have faced into the theological and pastoral questions of our age (same sex marriage, the ordination of openly LGBT persons, open Communion, responding to clergy sexual misconduct, the radical implications of baptism to name some), we have found ourselves guided by the poles of the tension between doing something new as a protest to the status quo and doing it as an act of ultimate obedience to a deeper aspect of the tradition's values.

Speaking as a white, straight male, I realize that my working life in the church has been very different than it might have been had the 1974 ordinations never happened. Here are five specific (and anecdotally unscientific) ways in which I believe that is so.

A recognition of the particularity of social location.   That I feel the need to identify myself by racial, sexual orientation, and gender markers at all shows that we are in a very different world than the one before 1974. I am old enough to remember a culture in which "white straight male" seemed to be the default setting for all professional life, especially in the church. Now clearly there have been a host of other movements in society and church that have lived themselves out alongside feminism in the intervening years, but I would argue that the leadership of women clergy and laity has been the driving force in our church's coming to terms with difference in all its aspects. Once men in church leadership had to recognize that their work could be done by others who did not identify as they did, they had to be open to the possibility that their own gender (and racial and sexual) identity was contingent and not absolute. In the years since 1974, the church has grown not only to acknowledge but to celebrate difference in ways that were unthinkable beforehand.

Words like "diversity" and "multiculturalism" and "privilege" are used now interchangeably to frame the difference question, and certainly the leaders of other groups (clergy and laity of color, LGBT activists) have been heroic in this work, but only the lived reality of women in authority made the church's engagement with social location possible. I rarely go to a church meeting these days without someone asking the question, "Who is not at the table or in the room?" We wouldn't have thought to ask that question in precisely this way had women not offered the church an alternative to traditional male models of leadership and authority.

New models for ministry.   Again, this is unscientific. But if I'm old enough to remember a church that was entirely male in its leadership, I'm also old enough to remember a church that had a pretty monolithic sociological definition of what ordained ministers looked like. In some ways that sociological definition was a product of the mid-twentieth-century "professionalization" of ordination. The changing of the basic seminary degree from a bachelor's to a master's degree, the introduction of standardized national ordination examinations, the establishment of continuing education institutions—all these developments seemed to derive from a desire to regulate ordained ministry as a profession on a par with medicine, law, and teaching. And the ordination process often served to advance those who seemed comfortable in a professional ministerial identity and to select out those who were not.

To my mind, one of the great gifts of the past forty years has been the loosening of all those stereotypical models of what an Episcopal cleric "looks like." The first thing I did when I was ordained a deacon was to get my hair cut. The next thing I did was buy a grey, chalk-striped Brooks Brothers suit. Neither my bishop nor I could have imagined my functioning as a priest in those days without fitting a well-defined professional image. What if I had shown up for my first church job with spiked hair, piercings, and tattoos? Today, though, we happily have clergy and seminarians around the church from an increasingly eclectic variety of cultural, ethnic, and class backgrounds, and they do not fit neatly into any particular model of professional or clerical identity. Our sense of the personal style appropriate to ordained ministry has broadened considerably over the years, as has our sense of the metaphors we use for clerical leadership. Is the bishop or priest a CEO, a teacher, a healer, a shaman, a guru, an artist? Sure! This decentering of clerical identity is a good thing, and I ascribe it largely to the lived reality of women in clerical leadership. It's a big shift to go from a grey-suited man in the pulpit to a rector who is nine-months pregnant. A church that can make that move can open itself to an even wider variety of clerical styles.

A reclaiming of Anglican pragmatism.   Though they seemed outrageously radical at the time, the Philadelphia ordinations now can be seen to fit into a continuous tradition of Anglican pragmatism. It is a deep part of our ethos to develop our theology from our practice and not the other way around. (*Lex orandi, lex credendi*: literally, "the law of prayer is the law of belief" often rendered as "praying shapes believing.") In 1784, Samuel Seabury (first bishop in The Episcopal Church) had to go to Scottish bishops to be consecrated because the English bishops to whom he first applied could not ordain someone who would not swear allegiance to the king. Seabury went to Scotland "irregularly," and his ordination as a bishop there forced both the English and the American churches to reform their practice to accommodate him and future non-English Anglican bishops. Seabury's action was controversial in its day, but by presenting the church with the fact of his episcopal ordination, the system eventually had to deal with it. Sound familiar?

Seen in the light of the process that gave us our first American bishop, the Philadelphia ordinations appear as yet another example of traditional Anglican practice: we act in response to a perceived or expressed need, we reflect and pray about the action, and out of the experience of action and reflection, we develop a theology that helps us get a sense of what God is doing in and through us. Praying shapes believing. *Lex orandi, lex credendi.*

Much of the change we have seen in the intervening forty years (same sex blessings and marriages, opening Communion to those not baptized) has been accomplished through this same pragmatic means. If, as other traditions do, we started with principles and then moved to action, we would not get very much done. We also wouldn't be Anglican.

An empathetic and compassionate church.   In the 1990s The Episcopal Church was one of many Christian bodies that had to come to terms with what felt at the time like a tsunami of accusations of sexual misconduct against members of the clergy. Some churches have been more successful than others at engaging this problem. On the continuum of responsiveness and transparency, I would place The Episcopal Church at the most responsible end. There is a reason for that.

As the complaints of clergy sexual misconduct began to come forward, the General Convention of The Episcopal Church, beginning in 1994, made serial revisions to its Title IV discipline canons. These changes not only made our processes more available and understandable, they shifted the burden of proof away from the accuser and toward the accused. (Remember: this is administrative, not criminal law. We're talking about losing a license, not life or liberty.) Before the 1990s, our church, like others, had tilted the process in favor of the cleric and often treated the accuser with almost total disregard. As the canons were reformed, the accuser was accorded both greater credence and multiple avenues to pursue an accusation should the complaint to the bishop fail. The result was not only greater accountability of clergy to their pastoral responsibilities and ordination vows; the result was also a broadening understanding of the appropriate limits to clerical behavior and an ongoing decrease across our church in complaints of clergy sexual misconduct.

I wish I could say that we were successful because of our inherent Episcopalian commitment to justice and compassion. The truth, though, is that in the end we did the right thing not because of our tradition of using Scripture, tradition, and reason to adjudicate church disputes. We did the right thing because our church had women in structural authority who would not allow the previously dominant "old boy" network to protect its own. Women bishops, women deputies, women on standing committees and vestries, women chancellors and canons to the ordinary—there were in the 1990s a heroic group of lay and clergy women who would not let the problem be swept away by the tide of Anglican squeamishness about appearances. Of all the many achievements by women in church leadership since 1974, I would place the reformation of our church discipline and sexual misconduct policies very high on the list. People's lives have been saved and healed and transformed as a result. The church is a safer and healthier place for everybody, even and especially clergy.

Although many male clergy at the time ascribed this reform to a "feminist agenda," I would offer a counter explanation. The women I saw leading this charge in those days acted not primarily out of anger but out of empathy. They felt with and cared for those (children and other women) who had been victimized by clerics using the numinous power of their offices to seduce wounded or powerless people to their own ends.

Though there is a long history of compassion and empathy as motivations for Christian social action and pastoral care predating the ordination of women, those two qualities have emerged in the last several decades prominently as warrants for our social and pastoral concern. To name just one issue, the current church drive to lessen gun violence in America—both in mass shootings and daily on city streets—arises out of empathy with the victims of that violence. Unlike other denominations, The Episcopal Church did not seriously start addressing gun violence corporately until the General Convention of 1976. I'm not claiming that women invented empathy, merely that the presence of women in church authority has made empathy a warrant for action defensible on its own terms. Beyond responding to sexual misconduct and gun violence, our church is leading the drive to face serious problems both at home and in the developing world: hunger, income inequality, and disease to name a few. We no longer need to give a reason why we care. We simply care, and that is warrant enough.

A preference for collaborative leadership.   If you've spent as much time as I have in church meetings over the last two decades, you will know how great a prurience we all seem to have for "leadership" in the twenty-first century. I ascribe this obsession partly to the larger culture of leadership in our business and academic environments. But at least some of the cause of this drive to develop dynamic leaders comes from an inchoate idealized dream of the individualistic, charismatic champion who can single-handedly arrest the forces of church decline we see all around us. The literature of leadership continues to construct it as a trait exercised by individuals. It rarely occurs to the writers of leadership books to imagine how communities might be leaders as well.

We seem to be at the confluence of two opposing trends in the church right now. For our purposes it might best be seen as the contrast between an increasing elevation of bishops (a trait I call on good days "episcopal exceptionalism" and on bad days "primatial creep") and other CEO-type leaders on the one hand, and the ongoing discovery of the egalitarian nature of baptism on the other. We inhabit a church that more and more at once exceptionalizes bishops and also insists at the same time that ministry be mutual. Talk about a conundrum!

The first trend (the "CEO-ization" of ministry) looks to the individual leader, the CEO or czar, who will size up the situation, figure out how to respond to it, and bring all the relevant people and constituencies along. This is the trend favored by the leadership books, spoken about at clergy conferences, and increasingly argued for by some in national church authority as the church reorganizes its national structure. The second trend (the baptismal track) is seen in an increasing preference for collaborative leadership. Outside the official church structure, there are several working groups (and I'm part of a few) that operate in almost a leaderless, "Occupy" kind of style. Not only are authority and decision-making shared; so is the hard, ongoing organizational work. I don't want to make an easy and reductive categorization of one style (CEO) as male and the other (Occupy) as female, but I do want to suggest at least that the perva-siveness of the second strategy has something to do with the way the church has increasingly discovered baptism as the primary warrant for all ministry, and that this discovery has emerged alongside the increasing authority of women in the church.

My crystal ball is clouded, and I do not have a clear sense of how this tension will finally be resolved. But I wonder at times why anyone thinks that strengthening hierarchy will be the answer to our church's problems in the twenty-first century. If I had to bet, I would bet on baptism. Even though we call ourselves the "Episcopal" church, our unique gift has little to do with our hierarchy. What makes us Anglicans is a shared commitment to prayer, action, and theological reflection all done in a community where all orders of ministry—laity, deacons, priests, bishops—are present, empowered, and engaged. Over the past forty years we have been privileged, as a community, to live more fully into this vision of who we are and what we are about. Our history and future are on the side of baptism and its implications.

So those are some of the functional implications of the ministries of both ordained and laywomen exercised in The Episcopal Church for the past forty years. As The Episcopal Church, we will always be called to stand in a series of tensions because we are, by our nature, comprehensive and pragmatic. The ordination of women as bishops and priests responded to an inherent, Anglican, creative ten-sion between advocating for equality and expressing the fullness of the body of Christ. The Philadelphia ordinations did not resolve that tension, but they and the ensuing ministries that sprang from them have shaped us into being more fully the church we have always been called to be and yet may even more fully become. We are both more equal and more fully Christ in the world today because we now function in ever more expansive, just, and compassionate ways. I will always give thanks for my sisters in ministry who continue to call us all into being the community God calls us to be.

THE VERY REVEREND GARY R. HALL is dean of Washington National Cathedral. He has served parishes and schools in Massachusetts, Michigan, California, and Pennsylvania. He is former dean and president of Seabury-Western Theological Seminary in Evanston, Illinois, and has taught at UCLA, Berkeley Divinity School at Yale, and the Episcopal Theological School at Claremont. He is a graduate of UC Berkeley (1972), Episcopal Divinity School (1976), and has a PhD in English from UCLA (1989). He and his wife, Kathy, have one son, Oliver, a writer and musician living in Los Angeles.

CHAPTER 15

Experience of Women's Leadership in the Anglican Communion

Katharine Jefferts Schori

Eve took and ate, and offered it to her husband. . . . (paraphrase, Genesis 3:6)

Then the prophet Miriam, Aaron's sister, took a tambourine in her hand; and all the women went out after her with tambourines and with dancing. And Miriam sang to them: "Sing to the LORD, *for he has triumphed gloriously; horse and rider he has thrown into the sea."* (Exodus 15:20–21)

"Grant me justice against my opponent." (Luke 18:3)

"Sir, even the dogs under the table eat the children's crumbs." (Mark 7:28)

Women have been leaders from the beginning of consciousness—learning where to find edible plants and leading others to gather them, and passing on that knowledge to future generations. That is at least part of what Eve is up to in Genesis. Like Miriam, women have led celebration, song, and lament throughout time, and tended to bodies before burial as did the Marys of the gospels. Women have challenged societal injustice with the tools available—with words and prophetic actions—the widow to the judge, the Syrophoenician woman Jesus engages, the suffragettes and women's rights workers over centuries.

Leadership means acting and agitating for change, and encouraging others to join the tensor field that indicates a different future, and in our context, a future that includes adequate food, community healing, and justice for all. The one called apostle to the apostles, Mary of Magdala, announces a different future for all creation when she proclaims Jesus's resurrection.

Women's religious leadership is buried deep in time—and the careful burials archaeologists have exhumed give evidence of their prehistoric care of corpses and souls. We will never know the laments and proto-prayers offered over the dead of those ages, but we can be certain women were deeply involved in affirming the sacredness of life and its circular or cyclical nature.

The Judeo-Christian tradition has had a mixed and divided attitude toward women as leaders, particularly as cultic (ritual) leaders. There is abundant evidence of women among the judges of Israel, as matriarchs of clans and nations, as deliverers of their people (Jael, Rahab, Esther), and even in decidedly nontraditional roles and actions (Lot's daughters, Rebekah as mother of Jacob and Esau, Rachel and her father's idols, Ruth and Naomi). Yet the formal religious leadership of Israel and Judah remained exclusively in the hands of men, and particular groups of men, until very recently. Women have always had a significant religious role in the family, including welcoming Shabbat and teaching children (and spouses!) in the ways of the covenant.

It's important to note the long tradition of feminine images of God in the Hebrew tradition—Wisdom, Shekinah, God imaged as a mother bear, and so on. The reflection of God's image in the full spectrum of humanity is more clearly evident in the Jewish tradition, albeit in largely separate spheres of life. Women religious leaders are evident in this tradition—the matriarchs, Miriam, Deborah, several prophets—Hannah, Abigail, Huldah, Esther—and in more conservative strands of Judaism, the rabbi's wife has her own well-defined role (rebbetzin). There are clear parallels with the role of women married to priests and bishops in some parts of the Anglican Communion today (and she may be referred to as "mama bishop" in some African provinces).

The formal religious leadership of women in Christianity is prefigured in the prominence of women among Jesus's intimate circle, particularly Mary of Magdala. There is good scriptural evidence of women as leaders of early communities of Jesus's followers—Lydia, Prisca, Phoebe, Nympha, deacons (1 Tim 3:11)—in spite of historic attempts to change or deny the gender of some! There is some archaeological and written evidence of women as ordained, liturgical (ritual) leaders in the early church, a practice that began to be extinguished when Christianity became a state religion in the fourth century.[1] Yet women continued to emerge as leaders—in the desert monastic tradition (e.g., Mary of Egypt), as supporters of Christian communities (Helena), as pilgrims and writers (Egeria), as leaders of monastic communities (Macrina, Benedicta, Clare, Hilda, *et alia*), and as theologians and mystics (Catherine of Alexandria, Hildegard, Julian, Teresa, *et alia*).

The patriarchal nature of much of human society in recent millennia has meant that only extraordinary or outstanding women leaders have been noted and remembered. Women have exercised religious leadership roles in three primary spheres: in the home and local community, as domestic tradents of the faith, through spiritual formation of children and households; in communal monastic environments; and although rarely until recently, as more public religious leaders, reformers, benefactors, theologians, and evangelists in their own right.

All of these modes of leadership are extant in the Anglican Communion today, in spite of patriarchal restrictions in a number of places. The Mothers' Union is one of the most powerful examples of women exercising leadership in societies where formal cultic leadership is closed to them. Across Africa in particular, the Mothers' Union cares for the least, lost, and left out, motivates male leaders to attend to issues of injustice and the need for change, and transforms communities toward a vision of the Reign of God. The MU is usually linked to patriarchal structures—the wife of the bishop is often the diocesan head, formal membership is usually restricted to married women, and traditional gender roles tend to be emphasized—but it nevertheless exercises an outsized role in transforming community life.[2]

---

1 For a brief introduction: http://ncronline.org/news/theology/early-women-leaders-heads-house-churches-presbyters.
2 This model of wifely support for pastoral ministry was urged on women following the model of George Herbert; see, for example, Louisa Lane Clarke, *The Country Parson's Wife* (London: Hatchard and Son, 1842).

Women's monastic life is a far smaller reality across the Anglican Communion, but can have equally significant impacts in local settings. Monasticism confronts cultural norms that expect adults to procreate, and has therefore not taken root everywhere in the Communion, but where it has, women's orders have had transformative influence on education, health care, and spiritual leadership. When the Mothers' Union and women's religious orders focus on educating and empowering women and girls through education, skill development (e.g., agriculture, finance, sewing, trades), and awareness of their full dignity as created in the image of God, they evoke a remarkable witness and engender profound transformation.

The great western missionary thrust of the last half-millennium really only began to significantly engage women in the nineteenth century, when some began to travel with husbands to non-Western parts of the globe with an eye to convert those they encountered. Ann Judson was among the first American women missionaries. She traveled to Burma with her husband, Adoniram, in 1812, and died there in 1826. She shared in the translation and evangelical work, and wrote about their experiences in ways that motivated others to follow her example.

Single women found encouragement in her witness and that of others like her, and by the late nineteenth century were being sent into mission territories at home and abroad to the point where they accounted for two-thirds of Episcopal missionaries. In 1889 the General Convention authorized the "setting apart" of women as deaconesses for ministry in both foreign and domestic environments.[3] Deaconesses worked in varied educational, healing and health care, child welfare, parochial, and pastoral ministries, with indigenous and indigent persons in cities, rural areas, reservations, and in foreign lands.[4]

The pattern of women marrying for, or into, missionary work continued. Charlotte Cox married her cousin William Bompass shortly after he came home to England to be consecrated bishop in 1874. They soon embarked for the Yukon. She was forty-four, he forty, and they remained in NW Canada until he died in 1906. She was responsible for carrying on the missionary work while he was out visiting and ministering among the people of the Yukon.[5]

3 http://anglicanhistory.org/usa/hcpotter/deaconesses1890.html.
4 http://anglicanhistory.org/women/deaconess1949.pdf.
5 http://anglicanhistory.org/women/bompas/index.html.

One of the challenges to formal leadership by women is the perception of inexperience—often the result of blindness to, or prejudice against, domestic and informal leadership that makes households and communities function and thrive. It has also produced something of a catch-22 for women who have not held formal leadership roles until later in life, when such roles first became open or available. Women who have been elected or appointed to such office are frequently dismissed by others for "lack of experience," which is often understood to mean "they haven't held formal office, so how could they possibly be qualified?" It also functions to keep women in traditional roles. The reality is that women worldwide have often developed leadership skills in local and informal communities, as well as in women's groups and societies, and they continue to do so everywhere. The Mothers' Union and similar parachurch organizations, as well as the formation provided in and by monastic communities and community development initiatives, all serve to encourage and equip women for leadership, both formal and informal. Anglicanism's traditional focus on education is an essential gift and resource for this work everywhere.

Today, across the Anglican Communion, women leaders can be found everywhere in the domestic-community environment. Monastic communities of women are still relatively rare in the Communion, but can provide important avenues for education and deeper formation for women in more patriarchal societies, especially for those who do not (wish to) marry. The emerging role of women as public leaders, especially in formal positions of authority, whether lay or ordained, is growing slowly.

Women were not permitted to exercise governance roles in many parts of the Communion until quite recently. In The Episcopal Church the first women deputies to General Convention were not explicitly elected until 1973. Yet in the last forty years three women have been elected to chair that house. Pamela Chinnis was the first, serving from 1991–2000, and two others have presided since 2006. A growing number of chancellors across the Anglican Communion are laywomen who have distinguished themselves as attorneys and judges, and whose experience and skill is welcomed by their dioceses or provinces. Rubie Nottage (West Indies), Sabina Boateng and Philippa Amable (Ghana), a woman reportedly newly elected in the province of Indian Ocean, Sheila Cameron (England), and Rosalie Simmonds Ballentine (Virgin Islands) are notable examples.

It is ordination, however, that has been the greater challenge, particularly for those holding theological positions that believe maleness to be of a higher order of creation (the "headship" arguments of some evangelicals) or ascribe a certain "taint" to the female gender (more often associated with the catholic wing). These arguments generally assert that since Jesus of Nazareth was male, no female can stand *in persona Christi* or act as *alter Christi*, thus women cannot confect the Eucharist or be validly ordained.

Some women—and men—have long asked whether such positions have developed in response to threats to the patriarchal status quo. The resistance to ordained women's leadership, particularly in recent decades, has been both fierce and intransigent, although once experience of their leadership is gained in local settings, much of the resistance dissipates.

In 1944 Bishop Roland Hall of Hong Kong ordained Florence Li Tim-Oi to serve congregations that had no other access to priestly ministry. Anglican hierarchs soon caused a sufficient fuss that she was forced to renounce acting as a priest. In 1981, toward the end of her life, she took up her stole once again and served the Anglican Church of Canada. This followed by some years the ordination of the second and third women priests in the Anglican Communion, also in Hong Kong, in 1971.

There has been a gradual expansion of women's ordination across the Communion since then, and it has accelerated in recent years. Today thirty-one of the thirty-eight provinces ordain women as deacons, twenty-eight provinces as priests, and twenty-one provide for their ordination as bishops.

The next province to ordain women was The Episcopal Church, which regularized deaconesses as deacons in 1973. Women were first ordained as priests in 1974, albeit extracanonically. Authorization had not been given by Standing Committees nor did General Convention vote to permit women's ordination as priests and bishops until 1976.[6] Women have been "regularly" ordained since January 1977.

The Anglican Church of Canada first ordained women priests in 1976, New Zealand in 1977. In 1983, women were ordained in the Anglican churches of Kenya and Uganda. Women were first ordained

---

6 Deacons were authorized in 1973, and former deaconesses were thenceforth understood to be ordained in the same way as male deacons.

as deacons in the Scottish Episcopal Church in 1985 and as priests in 1994; in Ireland in 1990; in Australia and South Africa in 1992; in England in 1994; in 1997 in the Philippine Independent Church; in 1998 in Nippon Sei Ko Kai; and in the Old Catholic Church of the Netherlands (Union of Utrecht) in 1998. The Church of Pakistan ordained women as deacons in 2000 (it does not yet ordain them as priests). West Africa (Ghana) made the decision in 2008.[7] In 2011, the Anglican Diocese of Cyprus and the Gulf ordained the first woman priest in the Province of Jerusalem and the Middle East, and another was ordained priest in the United Arab Emirates in 2012.

The trajectory for ordaining and consecrating women as bishops has been shorter and equally fraught at the beginning. The pattern has also accelerated and expanded globally in recent years. The Diocese of Massachusetts (The Episcopal Church) elected Barbara C. Harris as bishop in 1988. Voluminous and loud protests were made, but she was consecrated in early 1989. Penelope Jamieson was the first woman elected as a diocesan bishop, in Dunedin (New Zealand) in 1990. Jane Dixon and Mary Adelia McLeod were elected in The Episcopal Church in 1992 and 1993, respectively. The first Canadian woman, Victoria Matthews, was elected in 1994. Four more Americans and a Canadian were consecrated in 1996–97, an American in 1998, and one American each year in 2001, 2003, 2005, and 2006. In 2007, three Americans and a Cuban were ordained. The first two Australians took office in 2008, along with two Canadians. The year 2009 saw another Canadian, 2010 a Canadian, a Cuban, and two Americans; 2011 an American; 2012 two Australians, an American, and the first from Southern Africa; and in 2013 another Southern African, one American, another in New Zealand, another for Canada, and the first in the Church of South India, the first in Ireland, and another in Australia. In 2013, the Church in Wales voted to permit women's ordination as bishops. The Church of England is still dithering, though it appears that the necessary legislation will be adopted in 2014.

Today across the Communion forty women have been elected or appointed as bishop; two are deceased and eight retired. The pattern in the early history of women bishops has seen women placed as

---

7 http://www.modernghana.com/news/193743/1/first-woman-priest-of-the-anglican-church-ordained.html.

suffragans or assistants in far greater numbers than as diocesan bish-ops.[8] New Zealand is the exception, having elected three women, all as diocesans. Australia has named four women as assisting bishops; the first diocesan will take office in March of 2014. Canada has had three diocesans and three suffragans, and has just elected an additional diocesan (November 2013). Cuba has named one woman suffragan and one diocesan. The Church of South India named its first woman as what is essentially a diocesan bishop in 2013. Ireland named its first woman as a diocesan in 2013; Southern Africa's two women bishops are both diocesans, elected in 2012 and 2013. The Episcopal Church has elected twenty women bishops, nine of whom are or have been diocesans. In provinces where there is capacity for multiple bishops in one diocese, we may see this pattern continue. The Church of England seems to make a fairly regular practice of appointing men as suffragans and later translating them to diocesan bishoprics. The first and so far only woman to serve as primate in the Anglican Communion was elected by The Episcopal Church.

What difference have female clergy made in the Anglican Communion? Why does it matter to have women in this kind of leadership? Most fundamentally, the presence of women and men as sacramental, liturgical, and pastoral leaders gives incarnate evidence of human creation in the image of God. For the same reason that the church over the centuries has widened its understanding of the sorts and conditions of men who can give evidence of the one whose image they bear, the presence of the other half of the human race is a necessary correction to the tendency to make an idol of any limited or circumscribed imaging of YHWH.

Women often, but not universally, bring a more collaborative and participative style to their leadership. At least in many Western con-texts, educational patterns have shifted in recent decades to inculcate and expect that students learn these kinds of group processes, rather than an educational process focused on individualistic and competi-tive achievement. As a result, many sorts of institutions have shifted away from a rigidly hierarchical, top-down style of leadership. The church is often far slower in responding to the working of the Spirit as other human systems evolve. It is false theology to insist that only the

---

8 A similar pattern has been seen in placements of women priests—more often as associates than as rectors or solo pastors, particularly early in their ministries.

church can harbor the creative work of the Spirit, or that the church need never evolve in response. It is certainly appropriate to test the working of the Spirit, and as the early Christians were advised, "if this . . . is of human origin, it will fail; but if it is of God, you will not be able to overthrow [it]" (Acts 5:38–39).

In addition to greater collaboration, women's leadership has tended toward a broader inclusion of the concerns of all members of the community. Community development workers know this well, and offer the maxim, "When women are empowered, the whole community flourishes." This is a reality for women's leadership of all kinds, not only ordained leadership. Examples of this are legion: certainly work with prostitutes and orphans, and lately, concerns about birth registration in developing parts of the world—work that has been led by clergy and laywomen concerned about children who lack any status or recognition as citizens of the nation in which they were born.[9]

Ordained leaders, as well as empowered and skilled lay leaders, particularly in more traditional or patriarchal societies, often have greater access to political leaders and systems which can work to change social injustices. The gospel of transformation toward the Reign of God for all humanity and all creation needs the voice and active ministry of women as well as men. Our part in God's mission is to work toward reestablishing the image of human partnership in Eden, that we might serve side by side in caring for the whole of God's creation, and that we might be cocreators with God of a future that incarnates the divine intent for a restored creation—*shalom.*

KATHARINE JEFFERTS SCHORI serves as presiding bishop of The Episcopal Church (present in seventeen nations—in Europe, Taiwan, Micronesia, the Caribbean, Latin America, and the United States). Previously bishop of Nevada, she also taught at Oregon State University in religious studies and in fisheries. Her first work was as an oceanographer. In addition to scientific and theological publications, she is the author of four books: *A Wing and a Prayer: A Message of Faith and Hope* (Morehouse, 2007); *Gospel in the Global Village: Seeking God's Dream of Shalom* (Morehouse, 2009); *The Heartbeat of God: Finding the Sacred in the Middle of Everything* (Woodstock, VT: SkyLight Paths, 2010); *Gathering at God's Table: The Five Marks of Mission in the Feast of Faith* (SkyLight Paths, 2012).

---

9 http://www.registerbirths.blogspot.com/.